BATTERY NOT
A FATHERS DILEMMA

Battery Not Included
A Fathers Dilemma

Strategies for Strengthening the Bonds between Fathers and their Families

Robert L. Queen Jr.

**With Foreword, by
Pastor Neville A. Brooks**

RLQ Brand Publishing
Pittsburgh, Pennsylvania
Website: www.rlqbrand.com
Email: rlqbrand@gmail.com

Published in the United States of America

ISBN: 978-0-9988613-8-8

Dedication

I dedicate this book to my brother-in-law, the late George Brown Jr., a man who never had biological children of his own, but was a father and a guide to many. Some of his last words were, "Bob is writing a book that will change the world." Wow, I am indeed humbled by his affirmation, and must say it was an honor to share this vision for change with him. It is my prayer that this book will do just that.

George, I miss you my brother, my friend.

 Your imprint matters!!

Robert L Queen Jr.

A Message from A Father's Heart to Fathers Everywhere

A real father has a heart that is passionate, loving and kind. He has a vision for his children that spans a lifetime. He is not concerned about what he has or does not have, but will give his last to the ones he loves. He's not puffed up, but is open and strong and can always admit when he is wrong. A real father is not perfect but strives to be. He understands that he is like the roots of a majestic tree and his foundation runs deep.

As men, we are all born with the capacity to have a heart of a father, but we do not always have the example, the manual or the batteries. However, it is in our hearts to make it work and to push us to overlook the past and all the hurts.

Perhaps you are asking your own questions: Do I have the heart of a real father? Do I have the fortitude to stay and be the man who would not run and hide from this awesome, beautiful responsibility? What could be holding me back? Was it because I had never experienced or felt the loving embrace of a father or even had a fatherly guide to show me the way? Then you ask yourself one more question: Will I no longer let excuses and past hurts determine my future, my family's future?

So, brothers, my charge to you is to never give up and never give in. Keep pushing, keep working and in the end, you will win.

Acknowledgments

To my wife of 36 years, Georgeanna, thanks for all your love and support. Thanks for standing by me even in the tough times. I love you so very much. You are my heart and soul mate for life. The mold was truly broken after you were created. Thank You!

I would like to thank my children—JaNay, Rebecca, Robyn, and Katrese—for all your encouragement and love, and for pushing me to get this done. I could not have done this without you, please know that I love and respect you. As a father, I could not be prouder of each one of you. Thanks for sharing your hearts and hurts with me; it is helping me to be a better father and a better man. Thank you for your support and your forgiveness.

Mommy (Dolores Queen), this book is for you. I love you and thank you for inspiring me and for believing that this day would come. Thank you for seeing and saying what God said. My only regret is that you are not here to share this moment with me. I know you are watching and smiling. Rest in peace until we meet again.

Thanks to all my brothers and sisters, especially my big sis, Taunya, who encouraged me to go for it. Thank you. You each mean more than you will ever know. A special thanks to my Pastors, Neville and Connie Brooks, and the Jubilee family. It was very helpful to be in an environment where many books are being written and produced. To my editor, Gwendolyn Mitchell, what a God send! Thank you for bringing a great light and understanding to my words and thoughts.

To Katrese Queen thank you, for the graphic design on the book cover and web site, and to Georgeanna Queen for assisting with the reading and editing of the book. Dennis Pete, thank you for speaking into my life at a time when I needed it most. I was busy affirming others, but you saw the need to speak into me and affirm me. For that I am eternally grateful.

Dad, this is also for you. Although we did not have the greatest relationship, I have come to see you and the great things God had placed in you, such as having a strong work ethic. I saw you work, so I learned to work. I learned to see beyond the negative and see the positive. I wish you were still here so that we could come full circle as father and son, but I will go on and represent what a father should be, what you always wanted to be.

Most importantly, dear God, thank you for showing me the plans you have for me. Thank you for blessing me and giving me your strength, direction, favor and for being a father to me. Thank you for giving me the discipline to change my life and to help change the lives of many around me. This book is not about me, but has been written so that men everywhere will read it and walk in their true purpose. Not my will, dear God, but thine be done.

Foreword

Throughout human history, men have consistently been defined as hunters, providers and protectors of their families and communities. The roles of men were seldom questioned or debated, however times have changed. The roles of men have been blurred by a secular culture that has no regard for the principles of God. The biggest consequence of this revolt against God's plan is the erosion of the family because of Fatherlessness.

Thank God for *Battery Not Included, A Fathers Dilemma.* Robert Queen bares his soul to us as he tells his story of pain, suffering, healing and restoration, Robert shares with us how God taught him how to apply His word and access His power to become the godly father he never had.

Battery Not Included, A Fathers Dilemma will equip you to be the father God purposed you to be.

Neville A. Brook
Senior Pastor and co-founder of Jubilee International Ministries

TABLE OF CONTENTS

Robert L Queen Jr.

LET'S GET STARTED!

ON YOUR MARK, GET SET, GO!!

Introduction

"Fatherlessness is the most harmful demographic trend of this generation. It is the leading cause of declining child wellbeing in our society. It is also the engine driving our most urgent social problems (in children and adults alike). If this trend continues, fatherlessness is likely to change the shape of our society."

—David Blankenhorn, *Fatherless America*

Deep down inside I believe every father wants to be a great father. I do not believe that there are fathers who just do not care about their children. I am completely befuddled by the fact that 24 million children in this country are not connected to their biological fathers. In a rich nation like the United States, a nation supposedly built on Christian and family values, it is hard to imagine that the family dynamic has eroded to such a level. While I am concerned about all families, I am even more concerned about the families in my own community and about the men, both young and old, who find it difficult to assume their responsibilities as fathers for their children. What is stopping them from functioning in the most important role that they could undertake? How has our society encouraged the attitude that being a dependable father and reliable caregiver for your family are optional duties? As I searched for answers to these questions, I found a complicated array of hindrances and potential hurdles that create barriers even for a man who is committed to honoring his role as father.

We all have our own stories. Maybe you are not one of the statistics. Perhaps you are assuming responsibility for your family and you relish your role as father. Yet and still you have questions and want to seek help as you define and fine-tune your position in your household. You just want to be a better father. This book will help you to examine your strengths and confront your shortcomings as you strive to be your best self. It may also help you to guide and encourage another father. In this book, I will explore issues that confront men and oftentimes minimize the importance of their role as fathers. We will talk about relationships, baby mama drama, parental rights, child support, labeling the dead-beat dad, teen parenthood, pressures outside and inside the family, finances, lack of guidance, and more. Yes, these factors may cause difficulties; they must not be used as excuses to walk away from the responsibilities of being a parent. The lack of knowledge or the lack of training may be discouraging, however, this lack does not justify inactivity. Let your willingness to be part of the conversations in this book serve as a starting point to your becoming the most reliable parent and father that you are capable of being.

In *Battery Not Included,* I would like to speak directly to you as a man and as a father. It is not my goal to have all the answers. My goal is to provide fathers with tools to understand that they are the batteries that hold their families together. My questions to you before we embark on this journey together are: "How would you like to strengthen your role as a father?" "How do you view yourself as a man and as a father?" "What are the most important aspects of fatherhood?" "What is your vision for you and your family and how do you hope to achieve that vision?" You will have your own set of questions as well.

Battery Not Included

I am certain that this book will reinforce your capabilities to find the
answers for yourself. It is my prayer that you will find encouragement and
strategies for change in your quest to be a present, involved and caring
father who provides for your children both physically and emotionally.

Chapter 1

The Story Starts with You

"The enormity of problems like hunger and social injustice can certainly motivate us to act. We can be convinced logically of the need for intervention and change. But it is the story of one individual that ultimately makes the difference—by offering living proof."

— John Capecci and Timothy Cage

There are no perfect fathers. We all have areas in which we do well and areas we need improvement. If you are like me, there are areas that need a lot of improvement. There were areas where I was very unhealthy. I was a hurt, abused, seemingly emotionally dead individual, who was trying to be a husband, brother, father and son. I had not dealt with my issues, so I could not effectively deal with my family. There is an old proverb that says, "Hurting people hurt people." You never mean to hurt the people you love, but sometimes your issues outweigh your heart and your intentions.

You can never take back the hurt and pain you cause, but you can bring healing by taking responsibility and by building a better today and tomorrow.

The wonderful thing about history is that it is just that; history! It is a record of the past, but what you do with that record is what dictates whether you will be able to turn your life around and have a profound impact on the lives around you.

Let me offer a page from my own story. I viewed myself as a typical Black boy growing up in the inner city. But I knew something was missing. I was a confused young boy who did not have the benefit of a strong committed father figure in my life. Instead I witnessed issues of violence, avoidance, weak communication, intimidation, abuse and finally abandonment. I did not have a good example of the ideal father or a consistent role model to teach me. As I grew to adulthood, I internalized more negative traits than positive ones. I was not open to listening or receptive to others who may have been in positions to provide a different perspective. In fact, I was just plain not open; I could not hear, I could not feel and I could not move forward. I locked myself in what I thought was a safe place away from the hurt and pain, but what I had done was isolate myself from myself and from everyone else.

You see when you lock yourself away; you also lock the world and your love ones out. This type of isolation opens you up to failure, addictions and destruction. Eventually I found a way to address my issues and problems, but it was not easy for me or for my family. As fathers, we must first deal with our own issues. Many of us are afraid that we are not stronger than our past and we are afraid of being like our own fathers. We don't want to be the father that is not there or the father that is emotionally disconnected from our families. The good thing is that we can learn from our past. We must refuse to make any excuses for what they did or did not do. Also, we must not continue to blame others for the hurts which can keep us paralyzed in inaction. We have the power to be and do better.

BATTERY NOT INCLUDED

The reality is that we are the batteries. Our children need and deserve a healthy existence. They deserve to have healthy relationships with involved and committed fathers. Your issue doesn't take away your responsibility nor does it negate the fact that you are the father, and they are your children. As I share my story with you, I realize that my story is changing. I am changing my outcomes and I am in control of what happens next. I see my past can be a transcript of my future. I am a man of strong conviction, with a passion for change. I have been created for such a time as this. Now is that time.

This can also be your prescription for change, you decide. This can be your time to take a clear hard look as to how, when, and why you travel this journey to being a better father. I will tell you this; your children are the most vital component to the completion of your destiny. This is the time and place for action.

Grab a pen and let's get to work!

IS IT WORKING? TIME TO TEST THE BATTERY

Your assignment is to take time out to write your story. You have to come to grips with your story, the good, the bad and the ugly. What happened to you is part of your story. Who was there or not there is part of your story. The mistakes you made along the way are all part of your story. The way you got up when you were down is an intricate part of your story. Remember, history is a record of the past to be learned from and hopefully not to be repeated. Ultimately, you are answering the question: **"How do you view yourself as a man and as a father?"**

Please note: In writing your story, you may need to talk to a counselor to help you make sense of your feelings, hurts, deep rooted pains, and emotions. The biggest move you can make in life is one of forward progress. Here is an opportunity to get to know you. Enjoy the process.

We still have a lot of work to do. Will you join me on this vitally important journey, a journey to recover our greatness as fathers, our strength as families, and create a promising tomorrow for our children? If you're with me say I'm in!

****

Dear God, thank you for your power. I declare the curses of the father stop here, and the generational blessing will now begin.

Chapter 2

You Are the Father

"**Whatever your life's work is, do it well, a man should do his job so well that the living, the dead and the unborn could do it no better.**"

— Dr. Martin Luther King Jr.

We live in an era where men are not respected at a level that their grandfathers and great grandfathers were. In many cases, men have become the brunt and the butt of the joke. The term "daddy issues" is a commonly accepted term and is the focus of much conversation and therapeutic consultations. The fact is a large number of children and adults have daddy issues of some type or another. Recently, I met a man who was about 60 years old, who had major daddy issues, anger, bitterness and some true hatred for his now 82-year-old father. He has carried this resentment for most of his life. He also made a conscious decision to not let his relationship with his father determine the relationship that he has with his own children. However unresolved issues will surface in other ways, and until we come to grips with our deep-seated issues and emotions, we will never be whole.

Whatever the circumstance; whether it was not having a reliable father figure in your life or having a father that hurt you; whether it was having a father that abandoned you or having a father that was there but not there. These scenarios become the issues or baggage that you carry with

6

you into every relationship you enter. These issues however, do not have to define the future. You have the power to change it!

Somewhere along the way the role of the father has lost its meaning. The father is no longer the sole supporter and leader in the home. It appears fathers have relinquished their role as head of the household. The deterioration of this vital role brought with it a relinquishing of the man's obligation as disciplinarian, provider, spiritual leader, friend, confidant, and life coach and guide, rendering him ineffective. Still, who would be better to lead his children than someone who is responsible for their life and training?

Why are so many men unprepared to assume the responsibilities of being a father? Perhaps some of this is because many men lack training or have only seen inadequate examples of what fathers do. Many men and women are scarred by the memory of fathers who ruled by a punishing hand or negative words. They may have been negatively influenced by men who lead by making their wives and children subservient and fearful. Far too many families have been disrupted or torn apart by infidelity, which was dismissed and explained away as men will be men.

Yes, I had issues with my absentee father. I never had a man to show me how to be a man, and I messed up royally. Yet today, I thank God for an opportunity to have lived and learned to be a good man, a real man, a productive man. Deep down inside I knew there was a great man in there somewhere and that I had to bring him out. I had to move past the hurts and pains of abandonment; I had to move past self-condemnation and self-esteem issues; I had to move past the people I hurt along the way; past the drugs, alcohol, pornography, and womanizing, which crippled much of my life and the life of others around me, for so long. I had to move past all the things blocking my destiny and purpose. I triumphed over the internal mental warfare that held me captive, telling me I was not good enough, and

I would never be anything. Once I moved past peoples' negative words, my own negative words and thoughts, I was then able to see myself as a real man with purpose. More importantly, I was now capable of facilitating others to see their purpose and vision for themselves and their families. Instead of beating myself up, I now realize that recognizing my past mistakes and my past issues can now be a tool that can help many people, and hopefully bring out a positive outcome for men. I did not want to be a negative memory but an open book to be read of men, that they may see what God has done with this creation He has made. I am still not perfect and I fight the negative forces every day but I win now more than I lose.

Once we have confronted our "daddy issues" or other shortcomings, what is next? We get off course, guys, but like the Prego slogan says, "It's in there," and what and who you were created to be is in you too. So, let's go find him. Let's start by being the best you can be. It's a process. Move away from every negative issue, addiction and thought. See life the way you always pictured it but were unable to obtain it. You must see it before you can be it.

There is a movement started by a good friend, Pastor Neville Brooks and his team from Jubilee International Ministries, which I am proud to be a participant. The maxim is "You Are the Man." Yes, you are the man and there are no others in line that can do what you have been called to do. No one fits your DNA, no one has your imprint, no one can impact your children the way that you can, and no one, and I mean no one can teach them who they are, but the person whose line they come from. Others can love them teach them good values and affirm them, but no one can tell them who they are, why they move the way they do, why they think the way they think, why they have this uncanny desire to eat butter pecan ice cream in the winter time, only you. They need you to teach them who their people are and what their destiny is. You are the father. What are you going to do now? Break the generational curses of your father and grandfather and write a new chapter; one of success and destiny for you and your child. I know you can do it!

IS IT WORKING? TIME TO TEST THE BATTERY

Do you know who you are? You can't tell others who they are if you don't have any idea of who you are. You may not have been taught or mentored, batteries may not have been included, but "You are the father." What causes us to face the identity of our role as fathers? How can we live out our commission to teach, train, and direct the next generation? We live and learn by example.

Part One: Your assignment is to find an individual whom you consider to be a positive example of fatherhood and invite him to give you, an hour of his time. Ask him three questions:

1. What is the greatest joy you had as a father?
2. What was the greatest challenge?
3. And what is or what has been the greatest desire you have for your children?

Part Two: After you have had time to reflect upon his responses to these questions, take time to answer them for yourself.

***

Lord, as I seek to know what you desire for my life, allow me to speak with the heart of a father. Let me know my purpose and the purpose and direction of my children.

Chapter 3
The Seed

"Nothing Will Ever Be Attempted If All Possible Objections Must First Be Overcome."
—Samuel Johnson

How do you have frank and honest dialogue about all aspects of fatherhood without talking about sex and procreation? We know that the path to fatherhood does not begin with the birth of a child. It begins with why and how you enter a relationship. Do you ever think about the reproductive process and your importance in that process?

As I started to think about this chapter, I was focused on the word "seed." I liked the correlation between actual planting of seeds and the creation of life. What are seeds? Seeds are the thoughts that we have in our head, the ideas that become realities; seeds are your children. The seed is the symbol of your manhood. Seeds are the beginning of a process; they mark the continuum of life and much more.

Let me put a little seed in your mind. We were created to create life, to protect life and to live life to its fullness. In essence, we were created to make a difference in this world. And the biggest difference is how our lives impact our children lives. Our children are important and need to be grounded, nourished and protected. It is our role as fathers and parents to help them achieve their ultimate growth and full potential. The seed and its fascinating course through life have the making of a powerful story or a lackluster existence. The outcome is on you, the father.

As a father, you have an opportunity to start a great and wonderful journey with your children. Use the examples of your hurts, your follies, your falls, and your recovery, as lessons for your children's growth. Allow them to benefit from your story, don't hide it. Teach your children what you know and walk in your truth; be real and open, always be open.

Everything on earth has a beginning and ending. As the Bible puts it, there is a season for everything under the sun, a time to live and a time to die and so on. If we work under that premise, then we know we are on the earth for a season, a short window of time. What will history say about how you spent your time? Pretty much every reproductive cell starts with a seed, whether it is an animal, human or vegetation, it all starts with a seed.

A seed must be planted correctly for it to have a chance to be successful. We live in a day where the human seed seems insignificant to a large majority of today's society. The focus seems to be on the physical enjoyment and not on the preservation of life. Relationships and relationship building have been reduced to sexual attraction and physical connection. As responsible men and fathers, we must avoid the tendency to drop our seed anywhere, and with anyone.

I was watching a group of dogs once, three were male and one was female. Each dog was taking its turn trying to mate with the female. Each dog was from a different back ground; one was a shepherd, one was a mixed breed, another a pit bull. The female dog was a mix of a few different breeds. It did not matter to the male dogs whether the female was a poodle or a mixed mutt, it only mattered that she was a female and that they had an opportunity to release their seed. The male dogs had no particular relationship with the female, and it just so happened that the female dog was there at the time that was conducive to the male's call of nature, the need to mate. My point is that we are not dogs or aimless animals. We must not treat ourselves, or our partners in this manner.

How can we talk about being responsible when statistics are stacked against us? We live in a day where over 50 percent of all marriages fail, where teenage pregnancy is at an all-time high, where nearly 55 percent of all homes are single family homes, and where the biological father of the child is not present, or he is either incarcerated or dead. A recent U.S. Census Bureau survey indicated that 24 million children in the United States are not connected to their biological fathers. What I found in my sixteen years, as an anger-management counselor was that the most pressing issue for the young people was that they felt insignificant or hopeless. They did not know their identity and many were looking for love and acceptance in all the wrong places. What I also found was that many of their insecurities could be resolved through the careful and deliberant planting of the seeds of knowledge, and encouragement. We must value ourselves first.

Why am I so focused on the nurturing of our seeds, our children? If you knew that your seed was valuable and that your child could be the next President or Supreme Court Justice, maybe the next Preacher or NBA superstar, would you place their future in the hands of someone that means nothing to you? Or would you place them in the hands of someone you trust, someone who together with yourself will take that seed to its fullest potential?

I believe if we knew how important our seed was, we would not waste it just anywhere. Developing willpower is important because it allows us to forgo immediate gratification for long-term benefits. Think about it for a moment, how many bad relationships could you have avoided, if you had just waited. Fathers, the first thing I need you to understand is that your seed cannot be dumped just anywhere. Your seed is an investment in your future. Just as you are careful in your profession to choose the right place for the right pay and benefit package, you must be even more careful with whom you choose to carry your most precious seed. A job you can change if things don't work out, but who you connect with is a lifetime connection; no take backs.

Many of us go through life facing the age-old questions: What am I here for? Why was I created? What am I supposed to do with my life? The first thing you need to know is that your destiny is not just about you. It is about those connected to you, your seed or your children and your relationships and interpersonal connections for generations to come. We all have these questions. But it is how we answer them that make the difference.

A few years ago, I had the awesome opportunity to work at an inner-city school in a low-income community. During that time there, I met a young man from the suburbs, who was working as a teacher. His life from outside appearances seemed pretty good, but he was having trouble understanding children from this neighborhood and had trouble relating to their unique challenges. He said to me, I don't know what to say to them and I have nothing worthwhile to give. He knew he could teach them the fundamentals of math and geometry, yet he wanted to give them more and he did not feel equipped to do so. I encouraged him to teach them math because that was what he was trained to do. I also encouraged him to offer them life lesson: lessons of love, respect, trust and commitment.

I suggested he teach them from a caring heart, not a job responsibility. I suggested he produce an atmosphere of trust and respect in his classroom and demand that respect in return. It was his responsibility to show up with the mindset that he is committed to their success, the rest will come naturally. I was telling him to set the vision and make it plain, and to bring what he knew into the classroom. The greatest teacher is one that sets a course for the journey and invites their students to travel it with them. He had to plant seeds of responsibility and trust into each of those students, while being an example of dedication and truth.

ROBERT L. QUEEN JR.

A great secret to know about people is that no matter their economic background or societal standing, they all respond to four key truths: love, respect, trust and commitment. As a father this is even more important. Each decision you make impacts your future, and your future seed. This is true even if you don't have children yet. Your purpose is to use your gifts and talents to help others. I often think of my late brother-in-law George. While he left this world not having biological children of his own, he was truly a father and mentor to many.

Let's take another look at the seed and its natural growth process. In reality there are many reasons for a seed to thrive or to fail. The seed can thrive because it has been placed in well fertilized ground and in ideal environmental conditions, or it can fail because it was not cared for properly or just from natural causes. I like to use the example of a rose bush. The rose doesn't consist of just flowers with soft beautiful velvet exteriors, but comes from the earth with stems with thorns that push their way through the dirt and debris to receive the proper sun light in which to finish the growth process. From the spreading of the seed, to the housing of the seed, to the birth and growth of the seed, the right protection is very vital. Each phase if not done right can divert the life and destiny of that seed, and pervert, or kill its potential.

Where have you planted your seed, have you planted it in the palace garden, or left it for the birds to pluck away? Where you plant, your seed has a great deal to do with its outcome. Let me speak candidly to my brothers for a moment. Just in case you did not catch my drift, your seed is the most important commodity you own. It is your identity, your name, your future, and your destiny. It is more valuable than gold, money, houses, or cars. It is who you are for hundreds of years to come. Your name is so valuable that it will be carried on from generation to generation, in one light or another.

Let me leave you with a final story. There was a man who left his wife and family to spread his seed to another, resulting in the making of a son who was unloved because he did not fit in anywhere and who was angry and hurt. This son repeated the cycle by leaving his wife, repeating what his father had done and carelessly discarded his seed to another and another and another. His oldest son went about spreading his seed just as his father before him and his father before him, making a child with a woman he did not marry and had only known for a few weeks, leaving her to raise his child alone. Maybe if that first man had made a different decision and was there for his children, maybe the next generations, would have learned how to be there for their children. It only takes one generation, one man to make a change

The men I speak about were my father, his father and ultimately my-self, the son. We were caught in an unhealthy cycle of dysfunction. I now recognize my part in this cycle and am making steps to heal my family. I know from personal experience that this is not easy to do.

It is my hope men, that in reading this, you would do some self-reflection and make the life style changes that you need to change your life and the lives of your children and their children for generations to come. I hope we see now, that the passing of our seed is not merely a physical act of sexual release, but the careful planning of our destiny.

IS IT WORKING? TIME TO TEST THE BATTERY

Your assignment today is to plant a seed of compassion and concern. I guarantee the results will be instantaneous and the ripple effects unbelievable.

1. On your way through life today, stop long enough to smile and say "hello" to three people you never met. Wish them a wonderful day. Better still, ask them about their day and take the time to listen to their response. This may bring a smile to their face and may change the course of their day. They might pass this greeting on to the next person they meet.

2. Now let's look at it from a more personal and profound platform. Set aside some time to reach out to your own child or children. Give them a good word and wish them a good day. Imagine how they would feel if you spoke positive words into their life. Can you imagine the outcome of such a simple but tremendously impacting decision?

****

Dear God,

I know the tongue is the most powerful member of our body, a member that can give life or bring death. Help me use my tongue to affirm, to lift up and bring life.

CHAPTER 4

Bonding

"Most of The Important Things in The World Have Been Accomplished by People Who Have Kept on Trying When There Seemed to Be No Hope at All."
—Dale Carnegie

Brothers, we have spent a great deal of time talking about one of the most powerful contributions a man could give to this world, his seed or his children. In this chapter, we will address the importance and realities of the bonding process.

How are parental bonds created? It is often said that mothers have natural bonds with their children. A mother is connected through the umbilical cord to the baby through the placenta in the womb where it is housed for up to nine months. Dr. Miriam Stoppard, author and pregnancy health care guru believes that a baby first experiences the world through its mother. Her theory is that the baby not only experiences external stimuli but also its mother's feelings as different emotions trigger the release of certain chemicals into the bloodstream.

These chemicals then pass across the placenta to the baby within seconds of mom experiencing an emotion. So, if the mother is happy, the baby feels it; if the mother is stressed; the baby feels it as well. According to American Psychologists Association documentation, anger is accompanied by physiological and biological changes. When we get angry, our heart rates and blood pressure rises. The levels of our energy and hormones are also increased as adrenaline and epinephrine are released contributing to growing tension and causing blood vessels to constrict. This reduces oxygen to the uterus, thus compromising fetal blood supply. The Counselling Center for Human Development at the University of Florida agrees that anger can have detrimental effects on relationships, patterns of thinking, as well as, causing many physical problems, including colds, ulcers, asthma, high blood pressure (hypertension), heart problems, headaches, skin disorders and digestive problems in the mother and child. Another study suggests that stress in the womb could affect baby's temperament. Babies, whose mothers experienced elevated levels of stress, particularly in the first trimester, show signs of more depression and irritability (as well as being colicky). Research has also indicated that extreme anxiety during pregnancy could double a mother's chance of having a hyperactive child.

How you treat the mother of your child affects the development of your child. When a father is loving, and caring toward the mother oxytocin is released in the mother, and has a calming effect on the fetus. The fetus can feel the presence and love of the father through the mother. About the twenty-second week the fetus can hear and feel the outside world around him. At this stage, fathers can now directly influence their unborn child by talking to them, the use of a firm loving touch, or by playing music and/or singing to them. The National Association for Music Education suggests that selecting and playing music to your unborn child will help make better sound associations, which are critical for language acquisition once born.

This can also improve the child's fine and gross motor skills. Experts say, you should use classical music because of its range and calming nature.

In an effort to gain some personal insight, I spoke to a friend of mine, Paul, who always seemed to have a great relationship with his children. He said that when his wife was pregnant he would often touch her belly, and speak to his unborn children. He told me of how he would tell them he loved them, and how they were going to do wonderful things. He said that he did not know what to do, but in essence, he was speaking life into them. His father was never in his life, and all he knew was he wanted to do better by his children. I ran into his daughter one day, and can say, he did a great job. She told me of how she appreciated her father for being committed to her and her brother. Paul, like us all, just wanted to be a good father; but found out quickly that there was no operating manual, and batteries are not always included. His dad was not there to teach him, and he was just trying to do the best he could.

My brother Mark and I were talking about the title of this book, and he said that he sees it as "the batteries representing a power source, and we as men are the power source for our families." My goal is to help men understand our role from inception throughout the life of our children, and how important that role is to their success. Have you ever received a brand-new shinny toy car for Christmas, and there were no batteries to make it run; you wanted to operate it but did not have what it would take to turn it on? Becoming a father for the first time is just like that, wanting to know what to do, but not having a clue as to how to do it. How can I do what I have never been taught? The first and most important thing is being present. Be present from the word go. If you don't know the words to say, just be positive. When you speak peace and love into an environment, the atmosphere of that environment will change. When you come in to that environment stressed and angry, it affects everyone around you.

I remember my days as an anger management counselor. School officials could not understand how I was getting such a positive response out of the youth I worked with. Youth that had such a negative and angry outlook on life. I explained that I spoke positive affirmations into their lives, and that helped to change their world view. I created an atmosphere of peace love and acceptance. I challenged them to want to do better. When you speak life; you open doors of possibilities and tap into ones creative and directional compass, which I believe increases their self-worth and opens countless opportunities. Most of the young people that I worked with had no father figure and needed life's most important ingredient; love. A father's love, direction and understanding are keys that can unlock doors. We talked about the seed in the last chapter and how they are an extension of ourselves. How is it that we can get into new relationships, provide and care for our new children, and our biological children that are from a previous relationship are in need? They are living without the benefit of our time and presence, a critical key to their development.

Here is a model to go by; what you do for one child do for all. The time you spend on one child, spend on them all, be deliberate about connecting with them, so the separation of the past does not continue in the future. A good father will not just meet the needs of one of his children, he will meet the needs of them all. Bonding must be done on many levels. First with you and the baby's mom, whether you like her or not; there must be a level of care and respect. You must bond with all your children, raising them with the same time and care.

There must be a certain level of bonding and respect between your new wife/girlfriend and your former wife/girlfriend, so that you all are working as a team for the emotional, academic, physiological, social and economic success of all your children. It is time for us to put aside the anger, bitterness, distain we may feel about that troubled relationship, and make our children a priority. Positive parenting starts by creating a good relationship with your children, so that he/she responds to gentle guidance as opposed to threats and punishment.

The most effective discipline strategy is having a close bond with your child. Children who feel connected to their parents naturally want to please them. Discipline comes from the Latin verb meaning to teach or guide. It should not be rough, but firm, it should not tear them down but lift them up and train them to be strong and focused. When a father speaks, children listen. You must, however, be present to earn the right to speak. There is nothing that could take the place of your child's first word, first step or the first time he/she lets go, knowing you were there to catch her if she would fall.

In the later chapter on ages and stages of development we will talk further about the development of trust, a key ingredient for life on every level from academic, vocational to social. When my father spoke, most times it was negative, and for a long time in my life I lived under those negative words. I loved him, but I did not respect him, mostly for how he treated my mother, my siblings and me. I don't mean to belabor this point, but I want fathers to know that setting the right atmosphere is key to their child's emotional stability, and that starts with how you treat the mother of your child. Again, remember that every child is important and unique from the other and should get an equal amount of your time. This could be hard if you have a child who is passionate about things you are not passionate about, or who is not out going and just likes to chill.

I met a man today that told me a story about his relationship with his father. He was angry because the father never accepted him and had distain for him because he did not play sports like he wanted him to do. This man's interests were in math and engineering, in which he has achieved world notoriety. But his father to this day has never told him he was proud of him or told him he loved him. As successful as he is, he still has self-esteem issues from this relationship with his father and still doesn't feel good enough no matter what he achieves. I spoke to him in this manner: "Sir, I would like to tell you two very important things before you go. First and most importantly, on behalf of your father who is not capable of doing so right now, I'm sorry! I'm sorry for all the hurt, pain and rejection you went through. The second thing sir is, that I am proud of you and what you have accomplished. You are an awesome man, a great man." These were words he never heard from his father. I watched tears build up in the eyes of this great, successful and passionate man as he exited my car quickly.

Let me take time to say to every man, woman and child who has been hurt or rejected by a father, "I am sorry. I am proud of who you are and who you are going to become." It is so important to watch your child's habits and interests. You should work to make many of your child's interests your own or at least be familiar with his or her likes and dislikes. If you are not residing in that home, you should be in constant contact with your child's mom to find out what they like as well as spending the time with them to find out. This could be hard to accomplish but you must try and make it happen. (see the chapter on Baby Momma Drama). It may mean they like to read books, so you should see what books they are into and read and share that special time with them. Every child or adult I have ever worked with only wanted one thing, their father's time.

I met a young lady who was from a very well to do family. She was so unhappy; she said her dad was always at work and he never had time to spend with her. He gave her everything, a lovely home, whatever she wanted, cars, credit cards and travel to whatever destination she wanted; everything but himself. She said she began to rebel, cutting her hair from long blonde which went down her back to where she was bald on one side.

This made him angry with her and he would not deal with her. She then got tattoos and piercings over most of her body and he became angrier and refused to talk to her. As she sat with me she began to cry, she said I did all those things just to get him to pay some attention to me. My response was an apology on behalf of her father who was not capable or willing to do so at this time, I also let her know that I was proud of her and excited about what she is bringing to the future.

I believe there are two types of fathers, those who light the sparks of life and opportunity in their children and those who snuff the light out. Which one are you? You may not mean to, but your lack of attention, inability to communicate, or just plain absence, snuffs the light out. The bonding process is the most important part of relating to your child. My children know if they are in need that they can depend on dad to come through. I will defend and fight for my children, and that I have their back no matter what; but to be there to hear their hurts, opinions and concerns was not one of my specialties. I will say it took some work to get past this point, and we still have more work to do. I'm taking a very careful look as to what I did right and what I did wrong, and have chosen to share these experiences with you. It's almost like a pothole, every car will hit that hole if there are no indicators that will divert them from it, but when you see another car swerve to avoid the hole, most times the other cars are able to avoid the same hole. Warning pot holes ahead!

Bonding starts in the first trimester of your child's life. That's why it's important to be there from the word go. Bonding for the baby starts with the bond and care you have for the baby's mother, and the time you invest in them. Bonding is a life-long endeavor and is one of the joys of parenthood that makes you a complete and responsive father.

Is it Working? Time to test the Battery

Imagine you have three pieces of art paper, one red, one yellow and one green. Think about how you can use these sheets of paper to determine where you are in the bonding process between you and your child or children. Remember bonding comes from time spent with your child not child support paid.

- Red means you are at a standstill and possibly you are not in your child's life Perhaps you are too busy to know what their favorite color is and who their favorite teacher is.
- Yellow means you're around and know your child likes chicken nuggets and string beans, but have no idea of the name of their best friend or first childhood crush.
- Green means you are there for your child. You have a time that is just hers/his every week or even every day. You know what they like or dislike.
- You've met the best friend and you not only know the name of the teacher, but you help with homework and follow up with school every month.

Think about where you are in this process, then take the time to answer a few questions.

1. What color category do you fall into and why? Be honest with yourself. Remember this is a reality check not a criticism of your parenting skills.

2. What steps can you take this week to move from one category to the next or to enhance your relationship with your children?

****

Dear God, thank you for this great gift of life. Help me maximize my time with my children and to share the love and knowledge you have so graciously given to me.

ROBERT L. QUEEN JR.

Chapter 5

Realizing Your Importance

"We are what we repeatedly do. Excellence, therefore, is not an act but a habit."

—Aristotle

What would be greater than having a father who is committed and present in your life? The answer for many of us is, that we want to be or become the father who is committed and present in the lives of our children. What would we all give to have had that father, that commitment? What does that father, that man, look like? Who is he?

In search for answers to these questions, I conducted my own independent research. Over the last five years, I was able to interview and talk with several men who were prime examples of the ideal father and men who were not the best examples, but were willing to share their insight as well. Each had valuable tidbits to share. It was fascinating to hear story after story of fathers who listened to and understood their children. These men were responsive to what their children were going through, and met the emotional and psychological needs of their children. It was also helpful to listen to the other side and know that we all have room for growth.

Most men look at counseling as a stigma, a weakness and a violation into their private world. They view their homes and relationships like a Las Vegas commercial: "What happens in Vegas stays in Vegas." There are two very important facts I would like to share with you. First, if you don't deal with problems they will deal with you! Second, what goes into your body whether psychological, emotional or physical, will come out in some form or another! My point is that you should not be afraid to reach out to a professional. You are not alone.

I was not surprised to find that there were more similarities than differences among the men I spoke with. Many of the "disconnected" fathers had familiar stories that too many of us could identify with. They shared that their fathers were not there for them, did not affirm them, and were not role models to them. Many of them felt they made it out okay and that their children will also, but as I continued to listen one thought became very clear. There were a lot of unresolved deep seated daddy issues. As these men spoke, another point became crystal clear, many of them did not understand the importance and impact of their role as a father.

It is hard for you to be a light when you have never seen the light that you are predestinated to emulate. This is the core of the problem and why we are seeing generations of failure in the role of the father in some families, and generations of success in others. Where the father is present you will find children who become fathers (and mothers) that are present, and where there are a lack of fathers or positive role models you will see children who follow the same pattern.

As a father, you have been chosen to lead your family. No one else can perform this task the way that you can. Some of the greatest and most effective leaders are first great fathers. The call to fatherhood is not just to procreate, but to love, bond, develop, relate, communicate, educate, and to prepare your seed for their expected outcome. Think of the home as a workplace. As leaders in the workplace or in the home, our goal is to help our people to succeed. When they win, we win. No father or leader is worth his weight if his children or employees don't trust and respect him. Simply said, a man that is successful and does not feed his children or pay his workers is an empty shell who blows away without memory or thought. How can you lead publicly if you have no standing privately?

I asked each of the men to share some nuggets of wisdom and direction. I wanted to gain insight into their lives, but just as important, it was critical that these voices be heard and needed.

- The role of the father is to remove the debris and to create a smoother road for his children to travel.
- Good fathers are like good coaches. They motivate, encourage, care, and enable their players to be as good as they can be. Sometimes this involves direction, but mostly it involves removing the barriers to success.
- Some people say that leaders are born; others say that leaders are made. I don't know if leaders are born or made, but they are developed by other leaders.
- Fathers, who are good leaders, produce children that are future leaders.
- You cannot coach someone from the spectator's box; you must be hands on to make an impact.
- Your mission; which you should choose to accept, is one of great responsibility and weight. In fact, it is a matter of life or death, be a real father, don't talk about it, be about it! Be a father that makes a difference, dream it, live it, teach it, and help them walk it out.
- The call of the father is simply; show up and stay connected!

My Story

As a child and teenager, I never knew this "ideal" type of father. In all fairness, I truly believe that my father tried to show he loved me, but did not know how to express it. His interactions with me were often mixed with intimidation, threats, and burst of violence, yet that was his way. He was that "my way or the highway, I brought you in this world I will take you out" type father figure when he was there; and then by the time I turned thirteen he was gone from our home. I understand now that his fathering techniques or lack of, were due to deep psychological scarring that he went through as a child. But, let me be clear fathers, that no matter your past hurts or psychological scars, you must fight to overcome them and commit yourself to the child, the seed you have produced.

You must be committed to this excellent habit called healthy fathering. Remember your children did not ask to be here, they did not ask to be part of your dysfunctional environment. All they want is for their dad to be a dad and love them unconditionally. It was so refreshing to meet fathers who gave unconditional love, unconditional commitment, and who bonded with their children for life.

I must say, as I met these men and their children, I had a feeling of being cheated. Then I thought about how my children were cheated because of my dysfunction and deep psychological scaring. For years. my excuse was it's my father's fault, and that I was a product of my environment; as if that mitigated my responsibility for my actions or in-action. These actions were contributors to my thinking but every action in life requires a deliberate choice or decision. For the most part, we know the right things to do but choose to do differently.

When I began to get help to face the demons of my past, I began to realize that I was that thirteen-year-old boy in a forty-some-year-old body, I had never aged emotionally. I was that young boy separated from his father at a time when I needed his guidance the most. Although I was an adult making children, I was still a child myself. I realized getting the help I needed was a process, a process most men are unwilling to go through. Many people ask me what I would do differently. First, I would have never brought children into this world until I dealt with my own issues, and I would have gotten the help needed to function as a father and husband!

I would follow my now-known advice to be proactive about the dissemination of this most valuable commodity, the seed. I never knew and appreciated the great things about my father until I was able to forgive him and release him. I had to learn how to see past the negativity and find the greatness, which was in my father. By the time I figured it out he was gone.

Second, I would not have gotten into a new relationship when I have not fixed the problem of the past relationship. We tend to take issues from relationship to relationship, and it's always the fault of someone else. Third, I would not have been so careless about the lives of others in the name of sexual fulfillment. As Uncle Benny, would say, "An ounce of prevention is worth a pound of cure." Of course, I am referring to one of the Founding Fathers of our country, Benjamin Franklin. Fourth, I would be more involved with the care and nurturing of my babies at earlier stages in their life. If I was then ready to be a father, I would have bonded with my child and treated my baby's mother with dignity and respect from the word go.

I would do a lot of things differently. I would never have missed a day to value my children or to share with them my great heritage and culture. I would not have missed a chance to affirm them and watch them grow and thrive. Most of all I would be an open door where they can come to me when they needed a shoulder to cry on, or just to talk. I would love them unconditionally, no matter what choices they made in life. I would allow them to always feel my support and my strength, which is the greatest spear of influence we could have.

I would father with a firm but loving hand, and would never allow my children to be fearful of my anger. I would not hide the secrets of my past, but share with them how I overcame them. I found that when you deal with your issues, your children learn to deal with theirs. Just a side note: secrets destroy families. Open the skeletons of your closets and let your family heal. It is rough trying to deal with this, but there are many places to get help. The end result is closer, trusting, thriving relationships for you, your children and their children for generations to come. Healthy families and healthy relationships are born through openness and trust. If you want to end dysfunctional families, get rid of the dysfunction. It all starts with you.

There were many times when I asked my inner self, what is a Father? Well, if I go by what I had seen as a child, I would have a great amount of confusion. In fact, I would be at a loss for words. I loved my dad and I hated him all at the same time. He was present for one half of my childhood, and absent for the other. He was loving and playful in my younger years, angry and scary in my pre-teen and first teenage years, and then not present for the rest.

The first few years of my life were great. We traveled throughout the United States and Canada as military kids. I remember good memories like our own version of the people's court, crazy water battles, boating and fishing on the lake with my dad in his fishing boat. Somewhere about second grade the memories changed and life for us got scary. I'm not sure if the beating of my mom and the intimidation started then or if we started to be more aware of it, but it seemed like life as we had known it had changed.

31

ROBERT L. QUEEN JR.

There are events in my childhood that stand out for me even to this day. Like the time my father said I was nothing, and would never be nothing, destroying my confidence and self-esteem in the process. I believed his words; words spoken in a fit of anger that I took to heart as my life spiraled out of control. After all a parent speaks life into his children or at least he is supposed to. There were several destructive issues such as, drugs, drinking, women, sex and pornography as I battled role identity. I had no male directional compass; thank God for a strong Christian mother, who was a great mom, the best a son could have, but with all that, she was not a father. There were things that a boy needed that mom could not provide.

My anger toward my father was so intense, but was equally matched by my love and need for my father, which was just as intense. I was a ball of emotions without an outlet. Be careful of the power of the tongue, it can give life or become the breeding ground for isolation and death. Show me a child that does not think that they can do anything, who has no confidence in their ability to achieve, and I will show you a child who has been ostracized, demeaned, even abused by someone that should have affirmed them and spoke life into them.

My coping mechanism was isolation. Isolation from the real world, which caused me to live in an altered personality. A personality that came off as Mr. Cool-calm-and-collect, which worked well with getting the ladies but proved to create problems as I attempted real relationships with them. Relationships required caring, sharing and communication. This level of relationship was forcing me out of my comfort zone, to tell you the truth I was quite comfortable in my fantasy isolation mode, because I did not have to feel anything. I understood sex, but had big problems with commitment, I think this is why pornography was an easier world to live in, because it

32

was not real and could not hurt, so I thought, but in reality, it made relation-ships worse.

I was a father by age 19 in which I was not ready for. I did not meet my daughter until she was age nine. I also met and married my wife at twenty-two and had three more children by age twenty-six, which again I was not at all ready for. I did not even know who I was and had problems modeling to my children who they were to be. I talked a good game but taught from that "do what I say not what I do" mentality.

I mean I said the words but did not live by them, and parents let me tell you from experience, when your children find out the picture they believe about you is a lie, it is devastating and sends their reality into question. I remember a day when I took my daughter to a family reunion in North Carolina, things seemed well but suddenly, she bolted through the outside doors, and began to cry uncontrollably as the emotions leaked out about her disconnect with a family she wanted but, never had. A family she did not know and had not grown up with due to our disconnect. I was asking her to connect to a family she had been separated from for many years of her life.

She felt like a stranger, and even more so, she blamed me for not be-ing in her life, for causing this disconnect; and she was right. As I ap-proached her, I saw a 31-year-old woman reliving a time when she was thirteen-years old, who lost touch with her father when she needed him the most. She was scared to open up, scared to trust, and very angry as she stood outside on this cold December day with tears streaming down her face. I knew excuses for what happened were useless, and they weren't going to work here. All I could do was hold her, tell her that I loved her and that I was not going anywhere.

I knew the only thing I could do was to stay a present permanent fixture in her life. I'm still here and I'm not going anywhere, I said this to her repeatedly. If you noticed, I was thirteen when my father left, and she was about thirteen when I was disconnected, and so the generational curse continued. Things have gotten better, but I still have a lot of work to do, I love her and I know she loves me too.

Words of Encouragement

Fathers I strongly encourage you to turn off those inner voices of guilt and shame and leave the past history in the past. Let's open new lines of communication to our children and plant a positive in-print firmly in their lives. You can never recover time, but you can recover relationships. The greatest man in the world is not the man who never made a mistake, but the one who has taken ownership of those mistakes and seeks to make amends. In fact, the greatest antidote for change, is to turn a negative into a positive. When there is darkness, the best remedy is light. The greatest end to a broke season is to get paid, and the greatest most effective deterrent to bitterness and hate, is love.

You are the change you seek; it all starts with you. We live our lives seeking Power, Position, and Money, but the greatest level of power is to produce, develop and prepare your seed for an expected future, thus leaving an imprint and legacy for life.

The greatest position you could ever have in life is to be an effective, loving, present involved father. The payment is limitless. Do you understand now your importance? Do you see where you make a difference?
What can you do to make the change? Remember you were created to make a difference in this world. There is no one like you. No one has your

fingerprint and no one has your DNA. You are unique, you are powerful, you are important!

IS IT WORKING? TIME TO TEST THE BATTERY

Self-reflection: Your assignment today is to rate yourself. Find out where you are and where you want to be. Take out a sheet of paper and write down your goals. Think about everything from your childhood until now. What are your wants and desires, your visions, your plans and ambitions?

Once you have created your list, number them in order of importance and check off what you have accomplished. It's okay if you have not achieved much. It's not about what you did, it's about what you do now. Review your list and decide what will be your priorities for the next week, the next month and for the next year.

****
Dear Lord, help me to be a good leader with a plan of action.
Help me to be an example of strong leadership for my children.

CHAPTER 6
The Role of the Father

**"The Only Way of Finding the Limits of the Possible Is By
Going Beyond Them into The Impossible."
—Arthur C. Clarke**

In the previous chapter, we discussed the importance of fathers in the life of their families. Along with the collective insights on fatherhood, I shared a very intimate story of my own life and life struggles. Isn't it good to know that we are not the only ones dealing with problems and issues? I challenge you in this chapter to go beyond the limits of your past and to take your role as a father to a new level. I challenge you to go beyond the role of the modest Clark Kent status quo father and take on the role of super dad. Open the lines of communication with your children and become that super communicator.

Use your x-ray vision to look past their limitations and challenges and see their power, skills and passions. A French proverb states, "To believe a thing impossible is to make it so." I challenge you to utilize the mind of a super dad and go beyond the realm of impossibility and see into the land of all things are possible. The role of the father is key to the success and destiny of his children. Fathers are literally givers of life, no seed no life. With the delivery of the seed to the female species through sexual interaction, the role of the father has only just begun. Without a father a successful outcome is greatly reduced for many children.

A noted sociologist, Dr. David Popenoe said, "Fathers are far more than just 'second adults' in the home." He says, "Involved fathers bring positive benefits to their children that no other person is as likely to bring." Fathers have a direct impact on the well-being of their children and are literally proponents of their failure or success. Without intervention, the sins of the father are visited on the child. The first and most influential power in a child's life is the parent. The connection between father and child directly impacts the child's future outcomes, including cognitive ability, educational achievement, psychological well-being and social behavior. As we touched on earlier in this book, one of the most important influences a father can have on his child begins indirectly through the quality of the relationship with his baby's mother. A father who has a good relationship with the mother of their children is more likely to be involved and to spend more quality time with their children.

This family focused father will have children who are psychologically and emotionally healthier. Similarly, a mother who feels affirmed by her children's father is more likely to be a better mother. The role of the father should not diminish just because the intimate relationship has ended with the mother. It is important for both parents to understand that the priority and focus must be placed solely on the child. They must become a team, working together for the success of their child or children. "Teamwork makes the dream work." They are your dreams, your vision, and your destiny. They are an extension of you both.

The impact of a father is generational. Gifts, talents, abilities and knowledge transfer from generation to generation in the same manner as generational curses, behaviors and addiction. A father is a cultivator; he takes what is and develops it into what it can be, just as our Heavenly Father cultivates us from our sinful nature to His Righteous nature. A father that deals with his issues and habits teaches his child how to problem solve.

BATTERY NOT INCLUDED

Children with involved, caring fathers usually have better educational outcomes. Several studies suggest that fathers who are involved, nurturing and playful with their infants have children with higher IQs, as well as better linguistic and cognitive capabilities. These studies go on to say that toddlers with involved fathers usually start school with higher levels of academic readiness. They are more patient and can handle the stressors and frustrations associated with schooling more readily than children with less involved fathers. The influence of a father's involvement on academic achievement extends into adolescence and young adulthood.

Numerous studies find that an active and nurturing style of fathering is associated with better verbal skills, intellectual functioning, and academic achievement among adolescents. Involved biological fathers had children who were 43 percent more likely than children without fathers to earn mostly A's, and 33 percent less likely than other children to repeat a grade. Even from birth, children who have an involved father are more likely to be emotionally secure. One study of school-aged children found that children with good relationships with their fathers were less likely to experience depression, to exhibit disruptive behavior, or to lie and were more likely to exhibit pro-social behavior. This same study found that boys with involved fathers had fewer school behavior problems and that girls had stronger self-esteem.

The father has a unique role, just as scientist work to build or create the next best thing to take the market by storm, we too can be purposeful about preparing our children to change the world. You have the power to do so, it's in your hands. There is no more powerful sphere of influence than the role of a parent. This could be why you see so many parents living their lives precariously through their children, trying to give them the opportunities they never had.

ROBERT L. QUEEN JR.

It is my goal to show fathers that their lack of involvement extends far beyond the financial responsibility of their child. It impacts all areas of academic development and success. It impacts areas like teen pregnancy, drug and alcohol addiction, crime, incarceration, dropout, suspension, and expulsion rates, as well as joblessness, suicide, domestic violence, behavioral issues and economic status. The greatest most important deterrent to this is prevention, not creating children you don't intend to, or have the ability to be invested in for life. On the flip side, involved, invested, and dedicated fathers have the ability to turn these areas around impacting their family dynamic, social status, economic status and overall quality of life. Connected fathers bring healing to the family structure and changes the landscape of the community and the nation.

Fatherlessness is as much an enemy to our nation as any enemy we have faced in the last 240 years. The erosion of the family has led to the destruction of our communities and the weakening of our nation and its ability to compete on the national and international stage. Education is key; however, we spend more to incarcerate young minority males than we do to educate them.

This book is not an attempt to shame, beat down and expose the absentee father, but to educate him regarding his level of influence and his ability to make a change in this world. There are systems and generational hurdles that feed into this, and there are many reasons that cause disconnect, however, allow me to show you the short term and long term benefits of being a father to your children and the powerful position it places you in.

If you ever wondered what the greatest most rewarding job for a male is, it's being a father. Think about it, what job would allow you the opportunity to create and design the prototype of its most valuable assets, and allow you the opportunity to influence the outcome and usage of that asset for life? That position would be worth millions, but as a father it is worth far more. Face, it, don't we all wish for that one witty invention that would change the world as we know it? For example, the prototype of the first car, or the blue prints to design the first airplane. We live in a generation where travel by car and plane are the most dominant forms of transportation, and it all came at a time when the mode of transportation was by horse and buggy.

I don't know about you but I would love to be that person who changed the world for life, but wait, I am that person. I am the creator of that most valuable prototype (my children) and I can influence change for generations to come. We are all here for a reason and a purpose, and the role of the father is to lead and guide tomorrow's future. You are the change you seek! You stand in the gap between success and failure, between change and stagnation, between life and death. Weigh your responsibilities carefully.

IS IT WORKING? TIME TO TEST THE BATTERY

Your assignment today is to evaluate your role as a father.

- Are you leading your family?
- Are you visible, accessible, relatable and reliable?
- Where do you need to improve?

Rate yourself using a scale from 1 to 10.

****

Heavenly Father, make me the father you have purposed me to be. Let me be a light to my family and an example of your love, commitment and dedication.

The Reality Check

The Dilemma

The dilemma between fathers and sons is a silent lack of communication, continuity and training. If a door is closed, it would be very hard for someone to walk through it. When there is no communication, the ability to learn is lost. Access breads action, answers, affirmation, and accomplishment.

The dilemma is a faulty dissemination of information from one source to another. For example, imagine runners carrying the Olympic torch from one country to another country. The goal is to pass it to the next runner without dropping it. If the torch is dropped the fire goes out, and if it is not picked up and relit the succession ends. Just as with the fallen torch, there has been a proverbial silence between fathers and sons and daughters as well. The message is that the father is no longer visible or even relevant because of the lack of relationship. They are no longer speaking as one and the succession of information has stopped. The torch has fallen and the message has been lost.

The Answer

Pick up the torch, find out why it dropped so as not to repeat the mistakes of the past. The greatest attribute for success is finding out where you failed. Knowing how to recognize the problem is the key to a successful outcome. Consider the art of self-examination and look at yourself closely. Now ask yourself, were you in the proper proximity for this most crucial and vitally important delivery to occur, or were you too far removed to execute delivery properly? Proper communication brings about steadiness, which produces balance and permanency.

The bottom line is you must be there to take the message. Where do we look for answers? Why not start with the divine example of continuity? Jesus had a relationship with God. They had an ultimate agreement in the Spirit and they spoke as one. So, when you see the Son, you have seen the Father. The two agree as one.

Your answer is to carry the torch with confidence and authority and to agree about the final goal. Develop relationships with your family—the other torch bearers—and have that oneness of mind, oneness of spirit, and oneness of vision.

Chapter 7

Healthy Father, Healthy Child

> **"The remarkable thing is we have a choice every day regarding the attitude we will embrace for that day. We cannot change our past... the only thing we can do is play on the string we have, and that is our attitude."**
> **—Charles Swindoll**

In the previous chapter, we talked about issues with absentee fathers and the impact of those decisions on the children. We need to go a little deeper and talk about being emotionally disconnected while being physically present. Sometimes as a father or parent we can be there but not be there. We are so busy dealing with our hurts, pains, and who wasn't there and who didn't do for us, that we re-create the same type of scenario for our children.

In my situation, my father's father was not there for him. My father was not there for me. I was an absentee father to my first child and even though I raised my last three children to adulthood, in many ways, I was not there for them either. I was emotionally disconnected, therefore, I reverted to my learned communication technique, which was just "do what I say not what I do, my way or the highway" type of a communicator. I did not use active listening techniques, in fact, I did not use listening techniques much at all. As a result of my trust issues, abandonment issues, and issues of depression, I found it easy to isolate myself from my family both mentally and emotionally. Some days I would show up, and some days I was present physically, but absent emotionally. What I learned from this experience was that putting on appearances only muddies the waters, and your children know the real deal.

This is not a time though to run away and isolate yourself, but a time to deal with you. When you live a lie, you produce an unstable environment for your family. When you deal with your issues and habits, your family learns how to overcome obstacles. They understand that you are not perfect, and neither are they. Your family learns how to problem solve when you deal with your problems. But when you fail to deal with you, they learn avoidance as well. You see, it's all about the right attitude. Attitude! Attitude! Attitude!

You can change your world and your worldview by changing your mindset. I often refer to one of my favorite authors, Charles Swindoll, who states, "I am convinced that life is 10 percent of what happens to me and 90 percent of how I react to it." It is all about attitude and how you look at life. In matters like this, however, I am more inclined to turn to scripture. In his letter to the Romans, Paul teaches with this affirmation: "And be not conformed to this world: but be ye transformed by the renewing of your mind, that ye may prove what is that good, and acceptable, and perfect, will of God." The Bible shows us that we don't have to have a negative outlook, and that we have the power to change it. I had a problem asking for help, for years I felt I could work it out myself, and it wasn't until late in my life that I got some help to turn it around. If I had it to do over again I would have sought help for myself and my family long before this. Let me also be candid and say, I would not have gotten married when I did, because I was not ready. I love my wife, and know she is my soul mate and that we were destine to be together, but I needed time to mature.

BATTERY NOT INCLUDED

Get help for your issues, get help getting over your broken relationships before starting another. For your own sake, be there for your children no matter what. Wow, that's a juggling act if I ever saw one, but juggle you must. The best scenario is to get the help you need before you bring children into this world. I will be honest with you; I was resistant to any type of counseling and this almost caused me my marriage and my children. When I grew up, going for counseling was a stigma. In fact, to have a mental health issue meant that something was wrong with you. We were taught that if you were a man you handled your internal issues within yourself. You did not talk about it. For most men, if you asked us how we were doing the answer would be "I'm fine!"

Yet the reality for most of us is, "we are not fine. Experts say that mental health issues, are prevalent in over 50 percent of our nation's population. When I heard that, I was surprised because I thought if you had mental health issues that meant that something was very wrong with you, or you were "crazy." Mental health issues come from a strain on the brain, which could come from many different areas such as stress, abuse, loss and abandonment. It can come from depression and physical conditions as well as relational issues. Stress affects the body in adverse ways and can be damaging emotionally, physically or physiologically.

Mental health issues travel along a large spectrum, and can be minor to severe. In some cases, medication, may be needed. However, in other cases counseling would clarify why you feel the way you feel, and can be helpful in providing strategies, which can help deal with stressful situations. The most important thing is to identify that something is wrong and get the necessary help. Situations cause stress, and stress can cause emotional and mental issues. Many of these issues can be dealt with by talking it out. If you hide your issues and secrets, you destroy your children and family. It can also cause emotional, mental and physical issues for those that depend on you.

Remember healthy father, healthy child. It is not a stigma to go and get help, instead it shows that you are progressive and strong, and care deeply about the ones you love. It shows you care enough to end the cycle. It shows you care enough to stop the lies and secrets. It shows that you are man and woman enough to declare that the generational family curses end with you. You can stop the cycles of poverty, drug addiction, alcoholic addiction, smoking, womanizing, overeating, lying, pornography selfishness, isolation and so much more. You can end the generational curses of father's who were not present in your life, and be present physically and emotionally for your children. You are the batteries which make things run; you are the power switch which turns the lights on for your family. If you work to get healthy, you will give hope to all around you.

For a long time, my oldest daughter and I had some deep issues, and we did not get along well at all. We did not talk, and when we did it was not pretty, it would end most times with me shutting her down and not listening. An to be truthful my past issues caused many issues for her. In recent years, we have worked through some of this and have forged a better relationship, better but not perfect. Here is a post she placed on Facebook one year. "Happy Father's Day to the coolest dad around!!! Thanks a million for being there during the football games, band trips, relocations (Indiana, Texas, and Maryland), spider killings, family road trips and so much more.

Your presence and strength continue to inspire me to be my best self. Thanks for always showing up! Love you!" If I were to die today I would know that I was important to my daughter, and that I made a difference. This was a milestone for us which came only after I took responsibility for my failures got some help for my issues, and worked to change me. It's important that I stay healthy and be my best, so that I can continue to inspire my children. Fathers it a process and healing happens in stages but you must forgive yourself in order to be a conduit of healing and change for your family. They were able to go, because I was able to grow.

IS IT WORKING? TIME TO TEST THE BATTERY

"Healing waters" Healthy means turning unhealthy hindrances into rivers of holistic healing that bring about harmony and happiness to the inner soul, mind and spirit. Simply said, Healthy is a place of peace.

1. In this following assignment, you are to reflect on the negative words that have been spoken to you or over you and cleanse them out. Use the negative experiences and turn them into positive parenting. For example: "My father hit my mother" changes to "I have not and will never hit my wife, girlfriend or any woman." This is a modified version of replacement therapy. If you were called stupid, call yourself intelligent. If they told you, "you can't," you tell yourself, "I can." The power of the mind is vital. Who's controlling yours?

2. Be diligent about what you say to your children. Practice using positive words for negative experiences when interacting with them. Never let them feel less than, and never let them feel they can't talk to you. In essence, don't let them feel what you felt. Create a positive atmosphere of what you should have been feeling. Flip the script, be what your father should have been, but by all means face your own issues.

****

*Dear Lord, please give me the tenacity to stand and the power
to make the necessary changes to live out your great plan for my life.
May these blessings be extended to the lives of my family.*

CHAPTER 8
AGES AND STAGES

"You will come to know that what appears today to be a sacrifice will prove instead to be the greatest investment that you will ever make."

—Gordon B. Hinkley

The greatest investment is one that cost something. It is a sacrifice of your time and effort, but the dividends far outweigh your sacrifice. What you plant will produce something, thus if you invest nothing you will get nothing. I admit that I messed up as a dad, but I sacrificed my hurts, pain, embarrassment and comfortability to reinvest and reconnect to my children who are all now young adults. By coming out of my isolation, out of my comfort zone, I am learning who they are and who I am in their lives. We still sometimes don't always see eye to eye, but I can now look them in the eye and be real about what I feel and understand where they are and how they are feeling. I wish I was there or more open and involved when they were younger, and must say, I wish I had this book and this chapter particularly because it would have made a world of difference for my family.

In this chapter, we will examine Erickson's psychosocial development model and how fathers fit into each stage of development in the life of their child. We will talk about why it is important for the father to be there and active on every level. There is a mindset out there that the mother is the caregiver to the children and that a father's role is to provide and protect. I would like to challenge that notion, a notion by the way, I also shared. Let me share a funny story that happened to me and how I learned an appreciation for what my wife had to go through taking care of our children.

After the birth of my last child, my wife took ill and had to have surgery. She was on bed rest for nine weeks. Now that doesn't sound like an incredibly long time, but when you have to do everything from cooking and cleaning to taking care of a wife, from juggling with the needs of a 6-year-old, a 2-year-old and a new born; that nine-week period was a lifetime. I never realized what my wife had to do to care for our children, the house, and she had a job as well; Wow are you kidding me. Not to mention that when I came home from work, I needed her to focus on me, by night fall I needed her to step out of the pages of a Victoria's Secret catalog.

I had to change my narrow view of what my job was. I am so thankful for my mom and sisters who helped me get through some of this. If it wasn't for them I don't know what I would have done. In the past maybe I would get up in the middle of the night from time to time and pick up my crying child. I would, of course, occasionally help get them ready, but the bulk of the care was on my wife. That is how I always had seen it done. Well, welcome to the real world, talk about an eye-opening experience.

I remember taking my three daughters to the mall, I wrapped their hair in scarfs like a picture right off an Aunt Jemima syrup commercial and had the nerve to take pictures as a lasting memory of what I thought was a great accomplishment. When I look back on it, I see the clothes did not match, but they were the cutest little things. They enjoyed hanging out with their dad for the day at the mall. I gained a respect for my wife. Talk about culture shock. It became clear to me that I had the wrong attitude and did not make the right connections.

The mother's bond starts before birth when the child is literally a part of them. The great things about mothers are their normally unbreakable

52

bonds and focused connections with their children. They are not likely to just get up and leave when the road gets a little rough. Mothers stay even when it's hard for them to do so. The dynamic is different for fathers who can only imagine this type of connection: so, is it that women are stronger than men? Is it that women have an innate ability to bond with their children? Perhaps before I started to explore these connections, I would have answered yes to both questions. But it is not that cut and dry. I remember my mom and can say without a doubt that her strength got us through. She withstood the fights and issues of life and was there for her children. I had the greatest mother in the world. She stayed and protected and taught us through her hurts and pains, and they were many. She was committed to us; we were her life. I never thought that I would meet another woman like her until I met my wife.

If men would see their seed as a part of themselves, as an extension of themselves, they may have more buy in. Just as your child is a part of its mother, it is also just as much a part of you, in fact, no father no seed. As a father, you must develop an attitude that nothing is going to get in the way of your relationship with your child. The time and space you spend with your child has to be a mindset. If there is one common and important thread throughout this book, it is about being man enough to look past your issues and invest in the future of those that matter the most, your next generation, your seed.

One key way of bonding and connecting with your children at every stage of their development is, understanding the development patterns and needs of children. I would also like to go on record saying that as a young father, I missed some of these areas and wish I could have been more observant about the needs of my young children. Unfortunately, life gives no replays, no take backs, like a negative word out of our mouth, it can never be returned. What I can do is share what I have learned to help other fathers make the necessary changes, in order to foster connections and maintain ongoing communication windows with their children.

In Eric Erikson's Stages of Psychosocial Development, we find 5 unique levels of adolescent development. I want to incorporate a few points from a standard model used in human development studies. The psychosocial theory of development includes eight stages from birth through adulthood. The first five stages outline the progression of an individual's adolescents to their young adult years.

Stage 1.
Infancy: Birth to 18 months—Trust versus Mistrust.
Children develop a sense of trust when caregivers provide reliability, care and affection. A lack of this will lead to mistrust. We see it all the time in newborn and young babies. They will pull away from people they don't trust, and will cling to those that they do. It is an innate feeling they have. Have you ever seen a baby that will not stop crying until that mother or father picks them up? Others will try to calm the child but without resolution. However, when that child sees and feel the hands of their trusted parent, it is like all is well with the world. Fathers bonding at this age builds trust, stability and reliability, which last a life time and is their foundation for their future. This will only happen when and if you are present.

Stage 2.
Toddler: Ages 2 to 3 years—Autonomy versus Shame and Doubt.
We find that success leads to feelings of autonomy, but failure results in feelings of shame and doubt. Fathers help shape the child's gender role identity, they assist the child in gaining appropriate autonomy, which help's the child to identify and manage emotions. This stage is key for a child's independence and identity. Fathers this is done through positive play, and again your unwavering presents.

Stage 3.
Preschooler: Ages 3 to 5 years—Initiative versus Guilt.
Success in this stage leads to a sense of purpose. Children who try to exert too much power experience disapproval, resulting in a sense of guilt. In this stage, there is a great curiosity and openness to learning. Parents who take time to answer their preschoolers' questions reinforce their intellectual initiative. This stage fathers, is a wonderful place to talk with your child and help them understand the world around them, fostering a level of independence, an informed child is a knowledgeable child.

Stage 4.
School age child: Ages 6 to 11 years—Industry versus Inferiority.
Children need to cope with new social and academic demands. Success leads to a sense of competence, while failure results in feelings of inferiority, which can produce feelings of inadequacy and inferiority. Fathers, our main job here is to lead by example. Children mimic what they see you do, but if you are not there they have nothing to mimic. Children at this age will do what you do, therefore, it is important now for you to speak confidence and to reaffirm them about who they are and who they can become. Your encouragement will be key for them to overcome social, physical and academic barriers. Be careful here, if they see your anger, or negative behaviors, they will mimic this behavior as well. A child without confidence will shut down during this stage, and will mimic the negative environment around them. They will take their cues from what's available.

Stage 5.
Adolescent: 12 to 18 years—Identity versus Role Confusion.
It is important to have set the ground work for this momentous time in your child's life. At this stage, your child will make independent decisions. This stage is one where they will build social relationships. Dad, if you have been present, supportive, and if you have encouraged, and affirmed them, then you can sit back in confidence that they will be true to what they have been taught. This does not mean they won't make mistakes, but if you train, trust, support, encourage, and keep the lines of communication open, they will make good choices.

Traits of a good Parent/Father:

Reliability. Reliability is being someone who is present, someone they can trust, and someone who is dependable. Reliability is the ground under their feet and the legs to the chair they sit in. It is that feeling of security that is attached to the core of their emotional system and when they feel unsure they are un-nerved by it, making them feel unstable.

Care. Take an active part in their care. Learn your child's needs, letting them see your love and feel your touch. It's more than just words. It is the way they are handled; it is your response to the things they desire. It is the atmosphere you create around them that fosters their growth.

Affection. Everything from holding them and kissing their little faces, to your level of consistent play and laughter. Happy baby, happy life. There is something very special and different about a father's hug. It is like a security blanket which says your safe now, don't worry about a thing.

How you treat the mother makes a difference:

It is important to reiterate, that how you treat the mother has a direct impact on the trust and security level of your child. Try to avoid arguing and fighting with the mother of your child around your child. If you are angry or stressed out, you will channel that to your child if you do not appropriately handle or respond to the anger in a healthy matter. Therefore, you, the father, must set a loving, calm, positive and secure atmosphere to help foster healthy growth and development.

Direct Involvement:

Fathers play a significant role in fostering development in social-emotional, cognitive, language, and motor skills in the lives of their young children. Research shows that fathers strengthen development when they take an active role early and often in the lives of their children. An increased amount of father–child involvement can help increase a child's social stability, educational achievement, and their potential to have a solid marriage as an adult. These children may also be more curious about the world around them and develop greater problem solving skills. Children who were raised with fathers perceive themselves to be more cognitively and physically competent than their peers without a father. A noted sociologist, Dr. David Popenoe, is one of the pioneers of the relatively young field of research into fathers and fatherhood.

"Fathers are far more than just 'second adults' in the home," he says. "Involved fathers bring positive benefits to their children that no other person is as likely to bring." Fathers have a direct impact on the well-being of their children. Some fathers are under the impression that sending a monthly child support check is being a father, and that they are doing their part. Let me be clear in saying, this does not make you a good father. It is nice that you are sending money to feed and clothe something you created, someone who is part of your own body. After all, you feed and clothe yourself. This doesn't make you any more a father than the department of welfare. They also send a check each month. Does that make them a father? A real father is active in the life of his child. The biggest threat in our nation is not other nations, it is ourselves. You can change the nation just by taking your rightful place as a father. When you are involved things happen.

IS IT WORKING? TIME TO TEST THE BATTERY

Part One: Your assignment is to find what age appropriate stage your child is in and apply the fatherly love, guidance and bonding techniques needed for that stage. Remember every child is uniquely different. Know your child, their likes and dislikes, their dreams, desires and future goals. You want to be in your child's life? Now is the time to connect.

Part Two: Find an age appropriate event in your community and take them to it this week. Perhaps this can become a regular activity. Find time every day for a hug and an "I love you." Time spent wisely is like money in the bank. The greatest and most important appointment today is the one you spend with your child; all others are secondary.

****

God, never allow me to lose track of what's important concerning my family and children.

Chapter 9

The Twelve Core Strengths
of a Father

"Our deepest fear is not that we are inadequate. Our deepest fear is that we are powerful beyond measure

—Marianne Williamson

The twelve core strengths of Fatherhood produce strong, powerful, committed and focused fathers. These core strengths produce fathers who will stand and not walk away, fathers who lead by example and never make excuses, fathers who stay relevant in the lives of their children. The twelve core values speak to a father's strength, character, leadership, and to his ability to influence the lives of his children in a positive way. These core strengths are: Master Communicator, Man of Integrity, Honest, Leader, Teacher, Provider, Spiritual, Visionary, Servant, Man of Peace, Loving, and Dependable.

1. Master Communicator

A great father *communicates* in many ways. He speaks a loving word, showing his children that they are special. He speaks a soft word, which turns away wrath. A master communicator hears the heart of his children, and allow them to express themselves respectfully. A master communicator's most valuable trait is active listening. Be slow to speak and quick to listen, even if you have heard the story a

hundred times, and could repeat it in three languages. Listen, just take time to listen. You will learn many things about your wife and children if you take time to listen.

2. A Man of Integrity

Integrity is not just what you do but how and why you do it. It is literally the reason that you do what you do. Are you doing it because it is the right thing to do, or do you have another motive? Integrity is a man's lifeline; it is his legacy, a legacy that can be carried on in power and in truth. Integrity talks about a man's stature, who he is as a person. It talks about his character. Integrity says that you can be trusted to do the right thing, not just the popular thing. It teaches your children to have morals, values and respect for themselves and others.

3. Honest

The Bible has already set a standard for *honest* behavior. In his letter to the Philippians, Paul writes: "Finally, brothers and sisters, whatever things are true, whatever things are honest, whatever things are just, whatever things are pure, whatever things are lovely, whatever things are of good report; if there is any virtue, and if there is any praise, think on these things." This scripture teaches us to be open and honest with our communication. Secrets and dishonest words tear families apart. Having an open and honest heart brings healing and builds relationships.

4. Leader

You are the *leader* of your family and true leaders lead by example. A leader is a person who guides or directs a group. The term "guide" denotes influence. You have influence over others and you have influence over your children. If you want your children to have an even temperament, you must display an even temperament. They will do what they see you do. In the words of Gandhi, "My life is my message." Lead with integrity.

5. Teacher

A parent is the first *teacher* a child will ever see. The most important lessons a child will learn comes from his/her parents. You set the model for your child and you set the levels for learning and for living. When you are a strong father/parent teacher, your children become strong students, and eventually leaders and teachers.

6. Provider

A *provider* finds a way to feed and clothe his family; it is his number one responsibility. A good provider strives to meet the needs of his family, even if he himself has to go without. If your children see you work, then they will develop a work ethic, and recognize the value of hard work.

7. Spiritual

Your *spiritual* connection is your relationship with God. If you have no relationship with God, your personal relationships are likely to fail. If you build a strong relationship with God, you will learn how to build strong relationships with others. A man that has a strong relationship with God is more grounded and focused. A father must learn to love his children and others with a Godly love that is accepting and nonjudgmental. A father must love with a heart that recognizes the faults and shortcomings but loves anyway, just as God loves us unconditionally.

8. Visionary

You must have a *vision* for the future. Best-selling author Stephen R. Covey once said, "Begin with the end in mind." You need to see the expected end before you begin your journey. If you know where you are going, it is much easier to plan your steps to completion. Your children need to see you as a visionary. They will dream and have visions for their future, because they were raised under a visionary. They will have a plan for their lives because you developed a plan for yours. They will overcome obstacles and learn how to problem solve, because they watched you work through adversity and stay the course until the end. Fathers, think about the words that God gave to the Old Testament prophet, Habakkuk, "Write the vision, and make it plain." Articulate your vision for your life and the life of your family. Your children are watching and waiting.

9. Servant

The greatest quality of a leader is to be a *servant*. The servant leader seeks to help others and puts the needs of others before their own needs. A servant leader nurtures the leadership strengths in others and is not afraid to lead from behind. A good father/parent understands the importance of being available to serve others and will follow the instruction to put on his own oxygen mask before he assists his child with his/her mask in a crises situation. While the conventional school of thought would say save the child then save yourself, by placing your mask on first assures your child's success in mimicking your success. The father places the needs of his family over his personal needs and doesn't get caught up with his own issues/ desires, being in the front, but the concerns of those he serves.

10. Man of Peace

The Bible says, "A soft word turns away wrath." It also says, "Follow *peace* with all men". A strong father is calm in the way he carries his strength and power. He speaks and handles himself in a direct but calm demeanor when confronted with volatile situations. He says what he means and means what he says. He seeks to encourage and not to destroy. He seeks to build relationships. He holds his ground while respecting the ground of others. He seeks to hear the voices of others and not always to be heard first.

11. Loving

What is the greatest quality of a man and a father? The greatest quality is to have unconditional *love* for his children, and to have the courage to love with your entire being. The Bible teaches "greater love has no man but to lay down his life for another." God gave his Son that we may be saved and loves us beyond all our issues and faults. God expects fathers to have this same unconditional love for his children and his family.

12. Dependable

A strong father is *dependable,* trustworthy and reliable. A good father shows up and is someone who can be counted on to be available. A father's presence is not determined by the things that he provides but by his presence, his time, and his availability in the life of his family. A father should not just go through the motions of being there, he must find a way to connect emotionally and physically. A good father may not be remembered for what he bought his child for his or her birthday, but he will never be forgotten for how he picked them up when they fell, or comforted them when they cried. He will be remembered for attending that big game, laughing at a child's silly joke, and how he just was there when the world seemed so hard to navigate.

BATTERY NOT INCLUDED

IS IT WORKING? TIME TO TEST THE BATTERY

Your assignment today is to evaluate your strengths and weakness.

1. Take out a few sheets of lined paper. List the numbers 1 to 12 with several lines in between for comments. For each of the 12 core strengths of a father rate yourself from 1 to 5. If you are a strong communicator and your children agree, give yourself a 5. If you are weaker in an area, rate yourself accordingly. Please remember that a weakness in an area does not mean you are a bad person, it just means you have work to do.

2. Use the open area between each rating to make notes about areas you need to improve. If you receive all fives then you are the world's most perfect dad and I would love to meet you, because I have never met one of those.

3. On the flip side of that, if you have all ones, you may be too hard on yourself. Yet and still, you do recognize that you have a lot of work to do to be an effective father for your children.

****

Dear God, give me the vision to see where I'm weak,
and the strength to make the necessary changes needed to get stronger.

CHAPTER 10
Fathering with a Purpose

"It's not the will to win, but the will to prepare to win that makes the difference."

— Paul Bryant

Men of purpose produce children of purpose. As in Paul Bryant's statement that prefaces this chapter, it's more than just a will to win, it's preparing to be in the winner's circle that makes the difference. Preparation, preparation, preparation!

Purpose has no age or time limit, as long as there is drive and ambition you can fulfill your purpose. Purpose is driven by your passion. If you want to find your purpose, see what you are passionate about and pursue it. You must develop the ability to see the end from the beginning. If you have mapped out where you are going, it is much easier for you to get there.

So how does this translate to parenting skills? My mother had a thirst for education and developed it. She knew that one of her core purposes as a parent was to instill a love for education in her children. As a result of her passion, my eight brothers and sisters are all high school graduates and most of us are college graduates. We all valued education and have instilled this same passion to our children.

I am reminded of a nineteen-year-old young man from my high school, who had a learning disability and did not do well in school. He was encouraged to quit and get a GED, but he wanted to finish. He came to me and asked me what I thought. He told me that his grandparents never finished high school and that his mom and dad dropped out, as well his sister and brother. His passion was to finish school and be the first in his family to graduate. I encouraged him to stay. He was twenty-one years old when he finally graduated, but he stayed in there and made a change that will impact his family for generations to come. He realized that he was the change he sought. His drive for education and his goal to finish are why he succeeded. I believe he had seen himself walking that stage, and he did. He has now cast a new vision for his family.

Being a father with purpose allows you to take the time to see your most precious seeds grow to their greatest potential. It allows you to see yourself standing with them as they conquer the world in their area of expertise. If your father's father was not a great father and your father was not a great father, then break the cycle, be a great dad, in fact, be the greatest dad you can be. In sports a record stands until someone breaks it. Shatter the old record and start a new one, be the change you seek. If you can picture it, you can do it. You have to see success before you can achieve it. It is a discipline. You must see the goal then acquire the tools necessary to get the job done. You will never lose weight sitting on the couch watching the biggest loser or saying you need to change. The Bible says "faith without works is dead". This means you cannot just talk about change. Change will not come from your words, only from your actions.

I spoke to an elder recently about my health training desirers, who said, "Don't talk about it, shut up and do it." He asked me what my plan was to change my life situation with my health. He told me to enact my plan for success. As a retired military guy, he spoke to me about a preemptive strike. I knew enough about war tactics from my N.J.R.O.T.C days to know that a preemptive strike means you must hit the enemy before he gets a chance to hit you. He said if I want to be healthy, I must do the things necessary to be healthy. I had to look at myself, my situation, and the imminent danger facing my body if I did not make the changes to my diet. A preemptive strike is an all-out nuclear type weaponry used to destroy an enemy's capacity to attack. A preemptive war is one that is commenced in an attempt to repel or defeat a perceived imminent offensive or invasion. Simply put, I must begin with the end in mind, I must see myself healthy. I must do healthy things like working out and changing my diet to have the healthy outcome I desire. I must be the aggressor in the battle to eliminate the imminent dangers of distraction, destruction, despair, disappointment, and death. This type of aggressive planning produces, deliberate, dynamic, desirable dedicated dreams and discovery, which produces the diligence, and discipline needed to reach my destiny.

Fathering on purpose or fathering with a purpose is all about living on purpose. It's about seeing yourself and your seed successful. It's about seeing the imminent threat to your child's success and eliminating it. You cannot do that if you are not there. Are your children on your calendar of events? Are they in permanent marker or did you just pencil them in? The greatest leaders of our day are leaders that set an example and live by it. They are men who remove the stumbling block from their children's path in order to help them actualize their success. They are men who show up and stay no matter the pending storm, and are the same men who are still standing when the dust settles. Remember everything your child is, is because of you, and everything they are not is because of you. They are your DNA, a product of your genes, a replica of your image, a prototype of your design. Throwing them away is to throw away yourself, to throw away everything that you are. Father them with a purpose of success; teach them to be children of destiny and promise; help them make a difference in this world one step at a time, one moment at a time and one day at a time. Take the time to get healthy, be the best you that you can be, so you can be the best father you need to be.

If you ever thought that your presence doesn't matter, I urge you to think again. I don't care what the world says about the importance of the father and how insignificant you are to the process, don't fall for it. Every child I have spoken to about their relationship with their absentee father has been impacted negatively by the lack of that experience. This is a great day that we live in. It is a day of innovation and change. Will you be part of this changing world? Will you be a father that stays? Anyone can repeat a pattern, it takes a progressive, dedicated, visionary to set a new pattern! What pattern will you design for your children? What will your generational map reveal? Will it reveal a legacy of brokenness or a legacy of powerful men who stayed and built strong families and communities that mattered?

Is it working? Time to test the Battery

Living on purpose. Your assignment is to get a small notebook or journal for each of your children and one for yourself. Let's call these "Dream Books."

Encourage your children to talk about their interests, talents, dreams, goals and hopes for their lives. They also need to know that they don't have to share the information in their notebooks. This is their private space.

Of course, you can create times for sharing where you talk about what you are writing and about your goals for yourself and for them. This may open opportunities for them to do some sharing as well.

Tell them every day that they can do whatever they set their minds to doing, and be their biggest cheerleader. Most importantly lead by example.

***

*Dear God, show me how to be an encourager
to my children and family.*

CHAPTER 11
BABY MOMMA DRAMA

"Everyone here has the sense that right now is one of those
moments when we are influencing the future."
—Steve Jobs

"Start by doing what's necessary; then do what's possible;
and suddenly you are doing the impossible."
—Francis of Assisi

Love is care and respect. Love is the way you treat someone and the way you want to be treated. It is the most influential and powerful act that can ever be presented. Our mantra for this chapter is twofold. It talks about the ability to influence outcomes, but also addresses the gravity of that choice, a choice that is not so easily realized. When anger and hurt are infused into our emotions the outcome is bitterness. Parenting is a process that will take time and commitment, it will start with doing what's necessary, showing up when you're not wanted, doing what's possible as doors and attitudes become more flexible, and doing what may be impossible by working as a team for the good of your child. You can never get to the third step, the step of perceived impossibility, if you don't make that first step.

I became a father at nineteen years of age, I cared about my baby's mom. She was a very nice girl, who was younger than me and inexperienced. I cared about her but was not in love with her. I didn't even understand what love was at that time. So many of us enter relationships before we even understand what a relationship is, and before we know it, a child is born into that relationship. Here lies the problem; I'm having a child with you, but I really don't know you. At the age of nineteen, I could barely raise myself, so how could I raise a child? Now I have an even bigger question, who is this person that I'm a parent with? Many young relationships fail because they are built on physical attraction and a physical connection. It is very likely that critical information like a person's preferences and goals have never been discussed before sex is given. It is only after this exchange that the true relationship commences or lack of is realized. Unfortunately, it is too late and another child is born to a couple who is not in a relationship, leaving resentment, anger, bitterness and regret.

The greatest thing a father can do for his children is to respect the woman that gave birth to his child. It is because of her that you have the greatest treasures in your life. You may have moved on, but your children have not. If you can't be her soul mate, then at least be thoughtful, caring and respectful. Whom your children love should always be someone that you acknowledge with kindness. Your children notice everything and will follow your example.

My story was; I had no relationship with my first baby's mom, she was a nice girl, but we were still kids ourselves, kids who were playing adult games. We played a dangerous game which involved a new life. You see, it's the child that loses while you try to figure your life out or while you figure out that this person may not be the one you want to spend your life with. The reality is you are now connected to them for life.

Let me talk to the guys for a minute. Relationships for males and females are very different, just as our sexual organs are different. A male has an external organ he sees with an external view. What I'm saying is that he is attracted by the external view, the image. That's why when he sees a beautiful female, he can go crazy with desire or lust for her. He thinks he's in love, but it is mostly because of the physical connection. This seems like love until the next girl comes along. Gentlemen, women are very different. A woman's sexual organ is internal, they connect emotionally, mentally, and sexually from the inside. It's not just sex for them, but a love experience. When they lay down they want and need it to be meaningful and lasting. When a girl gives up her virginity, it's because she wants that relationship she has always dreamed of. When a boy gives up his virginity, it's usually a rite of passage, which tends to elevate him from boyhood to manhood. For some men, it may not be personal, it's just sex, but for a woman, it is very personal. Therefore, you should not become sexually active until you have invested a lot of time in getting to know someone.

With my first baby's mom, I did not wait long before having sex with her. While her dream was to wait until marriage, like most girls, my waiting time was about two and a half weeks. What followed was, we got pregnant! She went home to Los Angeles and I did not see her or my child for nine years. When I met my daughter for the first time, she was nine years old. We spent the next few summers together. Her mom and I, and the state had some issues over child support. She moved to another state and I was unable to locate her until my daughter was twenty-nine years old. I missed out on most of my daughter's life.

Baby momma issues are very real. Some are about the relationship ending, others may be over money or child support or needs for the child. She may not like your new girlfriend or wife, and may not want the kids to be around her. She may have moved and it is hard to get to her and the kids. She may have a new man, and she's okay with him being dad to your child. Her mom doesn't like you and is trying to keep you two apart. Maybe your family doesn't like her and thinks you can do better.

The courts are after you for back child support. There are many baby momma drama issues and reasons that fathers and their children get separated. You are not the first father to go through it. So, let's talk about the process of connecting and reconnecting to our children, no matter the cost.

71

ROBERT L. QUEEN JR.

If I had to do it over again, knowing what I know now, I would have gone to LA for the birth of my child and would have been more involved in her life. I would have filed for joint custody and had her each summer and some holidays. Yes, the state was asking for more than what I was able to give, and I still had to support my other three children and my wife.

Unfortunately, despite the issues, I found out there are no do overs in life. Once that time is gone it's gone. There are, however, lessons learned so as not to make the same mistakes again. I'm thankful that I can help someone else from going down the same path. I missed out on a lot of very important times with my daughter and our relationship has continued to be strained in some areas. I love her and she loves me, but "I love you" doesn't take the place of not being there.

It doesn't replace the hurt and lack of protection. It doesn't replace the encouragement that they need from us to survive. When my daughter was old enough to travel, I would have had her for the summers. This would have cut down the amount of child support and kept my daughter and I close. This would have eliminated all the lost and missing years. These years would have made all the difference in the world for my daughter and me. I also believe this would have helped her to have a positive connection with my other daughters and family early on.

If your baby momma is difficult to deal with, try to go through a mediator like her mother, grandmother, an aunt, or uncle, or someone who may get through to her for you. Be clear about your intentions. It's not about getting back with your baby's mom, it's about being able to be in the life of your child. Do not give money to appease them, keep track of all money transitions (keep receipts) and get a support order, or a letter of agreement. Do not give in to threats; get a lawyer if needed; some are free through neighborhood legal services. Do not enter an agreement that limits your access to your child based on what you give. If you give nothing at all, you should still be in the life of your child. No amount of money or lack of should be able to stop that. Please understand that I am not saying you should not financially care for your child, I'm saying that one should not be connected to the other. Let me make it painfully clear, a man who doesn't take care of and provide for his child is a man without conscious, dignity, destiny, and a backbone. What I am saying is that your time is more important than money, and that at any cost just be there for your children.

If you are not able to work out something with your baby's mom, again there is always the courts where you can file for partial or even full custody. This court order is based on the rights and care of the child, and has nothing to do with how much you pay. Therefore, if you need to, use the courts. Baby momma drama does not work in the court room. There are state laws related to the rights of unmarried fathers in relation to their children. The U.S. Supreme Court affirmed the constitutional protection of such a father's parental rights when he has established a substantial relationship with his child. Sir, fight for your right to be with your child, still being respectful and fare in the process, and they will grow up and respect you for it. Believe me, it is better than hearing from your child about how you were not there for them, and that you did not love them enough to fight for them. I need to tell you that even if you feel you had no other choice, it will not fly with them. All they know is that you were not there.

In the beginning of this chapter, I spoke about how women and men view relationships and sex. This information is vital to your success as a father as you deal with your children. Every view they have of you will relate to how you treat their mother. Every relationship they have with a future mate will be connected to how you treated their mother. Girls who saw their mother beat on, tend to find men who are controlling. Boys who grow up in physical abuse, tend to abuse or tend to be controlling. Men who treat their wife or baby's mom with respect tend to have children who have good character and confidence. They tend to be more balanced and successful.

The elders use to say "you get more with honey than you do with vinegar." Listen, whether you like her or not, she is the mother of your child, and there was a time when you liked her just fine, at lease enough to have sex with her, and make a baby together. You and your baby's mom should stay friends, for the sake of the children, if not for any other reason. Set clear boundaries, and stay within them, but always use respect and care when working with your ex-wife or baby's mom.

You are no longer a couple, but you must be a team. Separate your emotional issues about each other and work as a team. In your office, there are people you don't like, but must work with them to get the product or service out successfully. You both have a responsibility to the success of your child. This may also mean that you must attempt to work with her new husband/boyfriend as well as she, with your new wife/girlfriend. They are ultimately a part of the team working towards your child's successful development.

Partners for Life.

74

IS IT WORKING? TIME TO TEST THE BATTERY

Peaceful Waters: This assignment may be the most challenging task outlined in the book. Today, you are encouraged to begin the process of repairing the breach between you and your child/children's mom. Well, I will not say this will be easy, but it is necessary. Remember: "one step at a time."

Part One: Apologize, do not dwell on who started what or get caught up in he said/she said banter. Take the higher road. The important matter here is that you design an atmosphere that works for both of you to ensure the successful raising and emotional stability of your child/children.

Part Two: Make sure you are doing your part to help with your child. Remember your help is not just financial, although you must make sure you are pulling your weight.

Part Three: Take time with your child, which helps to take the load off your baby's mom and help you bond with your child at the same time.

Part Four: Get involved with your child's school. Get to know his/her teachers and keep in constant contact with them. Set time to help your child with homework, and be there to deal with behavior and discipline issues. This will help your child to be successful and will take some of the burden of your baby's mom.

These four distinct moves will show you are ready and willing to be a father, and will smooth out the relationship with your baby's mom. Remember, you may never be a couple again, but you are partners in the raising of your child for life. Respect her, treat her nicely and your child will respect you.

****

Father in Heaven, give me a heart of kindness and patience for others.
Allow me to speak words of healing and not of harm to all I encounter.

Chapter 12
A Powerful Connection

"The steps of a good man are directed by the Lord. He delights in every detail of their lives."
—Psalm 37:23

In Deuteronomy 6:5 we read, "These commandments that I give you today are to be upon your hearts. Impress them on your children. Talk about them when you sit at home and when you walk along the road, when you lie down and when you get up." The Bible teaches that the father was to be diligent in instructing his children in the ways and words of the Lord for their own spiritual development and well-being. The father who was obedient to the commands of Scripture did just that. In Proverbs 22:6, we are told, "Train up a child in the way he should go, and when he is old he will not turn from it." To "train" indicates the first instruction that a father and mother give to a child during his early education. The training is designed to make clear to children the manner of life they are intended for.

The command to love the Lord was given for us to love creation, for God is creation. We are commanded to love the land and to not defile it; to love one another and not to destroy each other; to eat healthy; to prosper, and be in good health as your soul prospers. From the first father Adam, to the present father, you, we must teach our children to love, respect, and to cherish this great creation, earth and our great Creator. What we learn from this is that a father is a creator not just in the planter of his seed that brings life, but he is the teacher of life.

A father's job is much more than a sexual act with his female counterpart, but the deliberate design and guidance of his creation, his children.

BATTERY NOT INCLUDED

God never intended the mother of your child to go it alone. Think about it everything in life was created in balance; night and day, winter and summer, spring and fall, and a time to work and a time to rest. Man, and woman each are created for a reason and purpose. One plants the seed and the other carries it. There are things the child learns from the mother and things he learns from the father. Creating a positive atmosphere creates balance and harmony and reduces stress, anger, bitterness, which can produce a well-rounded successful child.

When you are connected to God's plan for your life, your entire family benefits from that connection. Jeremiah 29:11 states, "'For I know the plans I have for you,' declares the LORD, 'plans to prosper you and not to harm you, plans to give you hope and a future." This plan is for you and the generations which come after you. I always say one man can make a difference. If you want to be an agent of change fortify your belief system, build a foundation of trust in God's word, work from your core and not your emotions, lean not to your own understanding, but seek direction. God's plan for us is to prosper, and have a future. Our plan for our children should be the same.

God never left us, you must never leave your children. God loves us unconditionally, we as fathers must always love our children, and remember love is an action word, so you have to be present to love.

The following are my thoughts about God's bridges to success:

1. Never discipline your child in anger. "And, ye fathers, provoke not your children to wrath: but bring them up in the nurture and admonition of the Lord." (Ephesians 6:4)
2. Teach them Godly principles through love, understanding, and respect by teaching and exhibiting the fruits of the Spirit.
3. Bring them up in the word, commandments and laws of the Lord. "And thou shalt teach them diligently unto thy children, and shalt talk of them when thou sit in thine house, and when thou walk by the way, and when thou lie down, and when thou rise up." (Deuteronomy 6:7)
4. Let them see you walk it out and not just talk it out. "Train up a child in the way he should go: and when he is old, he will not depart from it." (Proverbs 22:65)
5. Remember that your children are just that, children, and they will develop based on how you bring them along. "When I was a child, I spoke as a child, I understood as a child, I thought as a child: but when I became a man, I put away childish things." (1 Corinthians 13:11)
6. Lay the path and watch them follow. It all starts with you. Fathers, every path has a start and a finish. The importance is the journey along that path and how to equip our children for that journey.

Many battles do not have to be fought because they have been fought and won already, our job is to provide the map around the problem and connect them with the solution. There is no problem that God cannot solve. So, doesn't it make sense to connect yourself and your children to the solution. A strong man is a spiritually grounded man, who produces spiritually grounded and connected children and so on and so on and so on!!!

IS IT WORKING? TIME TO TEST THE BATTERY

Part One: Your assignment is to write a positive affirmation or message for your child/children. This message is to declare doors open for them and to encourage them in their endeavors.

Part Two: Encourage your children to pray every night and to faithfully adhere to God's Word, as often as you can, plan to join them. Be an constant example before them, they will mimic what your do. Build a foundation for the times you are not able to be there, for God is always present. Teach them to walk in faith in God's word.

Part Three: Affirm them daily as to what God says about them, that they are the head and not the tail, above and not beneath, remind them and yourself about what God said in Jeremiah 29:11, "'For I know the plans I have for you,' declares the LORD,

*****

Dear God, teach me how to pray, when to pray and what to pray for.
Develop me as a spiritual leader for my family.

CHAPTER 13
The Father's Tool Box

"You can use an eraser on the drafting table or a sledge hammer on the construction site."
—Frank Lloyd Wright

The proper construction of the foundation produces a strong steady building. The drafting table in our epigraph depicts vision and planning and the sledge hammer depicts destruction and starting over. Choose your tools wisely. The father's tool box is a set of specialized tools needed to operate successfully as a strong effective and involved father. A father, who is skilled in the use of each tool, carves out a powerful, successful outcome for his family.

1. **The Pick.** A tool used to tear down the walls of the past, making way for new growth and development. A father skilled in the use of this tool understands the gravity of breaking down walls and barriers that impede growth, communication and new development.

2. **The Shovel.** A tool used to evenly dig out the foundation for a great building. A father skilled in the use of this tool understands that without an even foundation the house will eventually fall. This is not a job for a spectator, but this job requires a daily eyes-on, sleeves rolled up, present and engaged type of father.

3. **The Flash Light.** A tool used as a search engine to identify hidden problems; a tool used to light the way for proper and lasting construction. A father skilled in the use of this tool understands its many uses. He navigates carefully with great vision and care; and he understands this may be the most useful tool of all because it identifies problem areas and casts a vision for the future. (If you want to truly see something clearly, put a light on it). See yourself as a successful father, see your children as powerful and successful individuals as you forge out a path for them.

4. **The Level**. A tool use to create balance. The father skilled in the use of this tool understands the importance of balance. He operates with a level head, an even temperament, a capacity to use active listening, and the willingness to change. This father takes time to see and hear the issue or problem then works in concert with his children and family to find a solution. He is not the "I am the father so do what I say" father, but he provides a format for dialog and growth.

5. **The Nail**. A tool used to hold surfaces together. The father skilled in the use of this item knows how to use everything in his repertoire to secure a strong powerful existence for his child and family.

6. **The Hammer**. A tool used to drive nails securely into the surface of walls, floors and other surfaces. The father skilled in the use of this powerful tool understands a stern non-threatening hand provides stability and leadership, not fear.

7. **The Screw**. A tool used much like a nail to secure surfaces and furnishings with a binding connection. It can have a flat or triangular head. The father skilled in the use of this item knows some situations need more time and a more secure unwavering foundation of love, patience and understanding. He understands that every child is different and learns in different ways.

8. **The Screw Driver**. A tool used to drive the screws securely into position and is made to fit the selected assembly. The father skilled in the use of this tool understands that it takes a steady hand and that a twist too hard can compromise the outcome and cause an unsteady foundation.

9. **The Drill**. A power tool used to segue through difficult areas making a way for secure devises. To use this tool takes a great degree of care and planning. The father using this tool recognizes that every situation is not easy to navigate. In fact, some situations seem impossible to break through. The father must be a master communicator in order to find a way to drill through the blockage, while not damaging the core of the structure.

10. **The Wrench**. A specialized tool used for tweaking and tightening bolts of all types and sizes. The father skilled in the use of this tool

knows there are sensitive hidden areas that need to be tweaked and tightened from time to time to keep their child moving in the right direction.

11. **The Ratchet Set.** Tools used to secure a variety of bolts in hard to reach areas and further securing the foundation. The father skilled in this area knows it takes patience, teamwork, dedication, devotion, connection, hands-on involvement, and understanding. He knows it takes the ability to see deeper, listen more carefully, and love unconditionally. He understands that his investment is for a lifetime not a nighttime.

12. **The Compass.** Every good handyman also has a compass that does two things: it sets the right direction to proceed, and it helps to keep you and your children/family moving in a forward motion. The most important things to understand about a compass is that you need to have one. If your morals and values are in question, you will not have success teaching the right ones to your children. They will often imitate what you do, and even if they don't wish to, they will do what they see done. It's called learned behavior.

13. **The Measuring Tape.** Another key tool in the father's tool box, the measuring tape, unlike any other tool, has a powerful significance because it gages and assesses growth. Sometimes growth is the hardest area to measure because, some growth is outwardly evident and some growth takes years to manifest. In some cases, you won't see that growth until your son becomes a father or your daughter becomes a mother. This tool is key in the area of vision casting that prepares them for the world systems, and helps them overcome obstacles along their journey as well as help sharpen their tools to navigate the road ahead.

14. **The Pocket Knife.** A multipurpose tool that has a foldable knife that fits inside the handle and fits neatly in a pocket. This tool is used to show you are always prepared. A father skilled in this area has the steadiness of a surgeon and is skilled in cutting out the negative issue without damaging the object or the child. A Father using this tool shows that he has ingenuity to solve all kinds of problems.

Using the Father's Tool Box

If you had the opportunity to build a model of a great father, what would that look like? The father's tool box has given you a breakdown of the tools necessary to complete this process. As part of your preparation make sure your package has all the tools listed. Proper preparation is paramount to your success. No handyman goes on the job without his tool box and tools.

So, what would preparation look like for the role of the father? This role starts with introspection. Before you can lead, you must evaluate your ability to lead. Before a person can go to work in this area he must subscribe to a certain process. This type of preparation includes physical, mental, emotional, and spiritual evaluation of one's personal willingness to change and develop.

Do you possess the tools needed to be a great father? Let's answer a few very important questions from the handyman's checklist or preparation questionnaire. These questions will help you develop your own instructional manual or step-by-step guide to the proper shaping of the model father. Please consider each question carefully before starting the next.

The Handyman's Checklist and Preparation Questionnaire

1. What is my worldview of what a father is and how should I operate in this prestigious role?
2. What is my personal vision for success and how have I prepared for it?
3. Have I dealt with all my own issues or daddy issues and the mental, emotional and psychological fall out from those issues?
4. Have I educated myself on this role and its requirements and expectations?

5. Am I healthy physically, mentally, emotionally, financially and spiritually to accept this responsibility?
6. Am I willing to step into the role for a lifetime?
7. Have I picked the right partner to share this role?
8. How much do I know about her? Is she someone I want to be with for a night time (i.e. physical attraction) or a lifetime (wife/ mother potential)?
9. What is her relationship or view of her father or fathers in general?
10. Has she dealt with all of her daddy issues and their mental, emotional, and or psychological fallout?
11. What is her reasoning for picking you?
12. How does she see her future? Is she a person with a vision for success; and is she prepared or preparing for that goal?
13. Does her vision for success match yours?
14. How do you and your potential partner see your children's success? What have you done to prepare for their life in a world of so many pitfalls?
15. How will you train your children? Do you both agree?
16. What type of counseling have you and your potential partner gone through to be prepared?
17. How many books have you and your potential partner read on the subject?
18. What do you know about the stages of a child's development?

WARNING:
Failure to follow all instructions or answer each question could result in the death of your seed, your vision and your destiny!

Every one of these questions must be given great consideration before you bring a child into this world. Failure to do so, could give us more of the same hurt, emotionally bankrupt, physically challenged, poor, lost, uneducated, and fatherless children of which there are 24 million in the United States alone. You may have already brought a child or children into this world and may not have done your due diligence for yourself or your children. You may not be in a good relationship, but the outcomes can still be achieved through respect and working together for the success of your children. It's not too late to help your children make those inroads to success by preparing yourself to jump back into that vitally important role. We look at this world and complain about its outcomes and attitudes, when all the while we hold the keys to change. The first key to that change is preparation.

IS IT WORKING? TIME TO TEST THE BATTERY

1. Take time to evaluate your tool box, do you possess the tools necessary to be an effective father/parent right now?

2. Have you answered the preparation questionnaire, and have you chosen wisely?

3. If your answer is no, what is your plan to turn it around?

4. What have you learned from the process?

5. What tool or tools do you need to develop?

6. What is your vision for you and your children/family?

The greatest thing about the battle is the victory celebration. I encourage you to never give up. Yes, you will have failures along the way, but if you stay focused you will have more successes than you will have failures. Remember, if you have a vision for the future, good preparation, a powerful spiritual connection and the right tools, you will never be alone.

****

Trust in God.
He will show you how to apply these great keys to your life,
and will give you a glimpse of the outcome,
an outcome that shows you winning!

Chapter 14
The Final Word

"The final test of a leader is that he leaves behind him in other men the conviction and the will to carry on."

- Walter Lippmann

Your child, your seed, is waiting for you to love it, care for it, and direct it to its most important future. The bottom line brothers are no one can do what you do. I believe with everything in my heart that fathers are not only important, but they are a vital source of direction and survival for our children. Unfortunately, not having fathers in their most important role for so long has become normal rather than abnormal. I have heard fathers say, "My children will be okay, my dad was not there for me and I came out okay." My question for them is: "did you?" Seven failed relationships later, unrealized dreams and vision, and a directional compass which is all over the place: "Did you really? Are you really okay?"

At the start of this book I shared my surprise about the notion that fathers don't care, and how I was totally shocked by the fact that 24 million children are not connected to their bio-logical father; I just did not understand it. I am still taken back by these daunting and breath-taking numbers. I am also dismayed by the amount of teen pregnancies, teen suicide, teen murders, and teen and adult incarceration and addictions. Fathers, will they really be okay without you? We have become desensitized by these facts and statistics; and we have accepted the mindset that life happens and there is nothing we can do about it. But I beg to differ. You can change it. You can restore hope to an apparently hopeless situation, because nothing is hopeless.

BATTERY NOT INCLUDED

I'm not saying it will be easy, however it is necessary to give your children a positive outcome. You may not be accepted at first, but don't go away. Keep fighting for them; you will be glad you did. You see, fathers, you are the change you seek. You are the light that brightens up their tomorrow, and the directional compose which leads them to a positive destiny.

I can be in despair about not being there for most of my one daughter's life, and being emotionally absent in the lives of my other three daughters. I can dwell in my hurt, and the hurt I caused others, I can sit around licking my wounds and complaining about milk that has been spilled, or I can do something about it. I chose to win! As long as there is life, there is hope and because of that I now have a better relationship with all my daughters. Is it the best relationship? To be honest, no, but we are in a good place and we are working on it daily. No, I did not change the past, however, I have cleaned up the spilled milk by showing up, and by taking responsibility for my mistakes and working every day to change what was, to what it could be. The spilled milk of life may never be forgotten, however, neither will your dedication to change for the better.

I remember, one day I was at a meeting with my good friends, Ray and Mr. Pete, when a young man ran past the door. He was being pursued by three others behind him and then five shots rang out. My friend, Mr. Pete, ran to the door and yelled, "Man down!" I ran out of the restaurant and was the first to get to this young man. I was there as he took his final breaths and left this world. I began to cry for this young man, whom I did not know, and promised myself, I would do everything in my power to make sure this did not happen again. Since that day, I have been blessed to speak into the lives of over four thousand children and countless adults. Yet when I consider the millions of children lost and in despair, I know I have not even scratched the surface. There was one message that rang out in nearly every mentoring, counseling and ministry session, and that was in the words of a great young singer song writer, Donavan: "It sure would be nice to have my father around."

I wrote this book because I truly believe that one man can make a difference. But, fathers, together we can make a change. Start with your children, and then reach out to others. If we can reconnect millions of children just by starting at home, this world would be a completely different place. Fathers make the difference. I challenge you today to find your child or children and reach out to them. Never give up. Make them number one on your list. Design your time around them and find a way to reach them. I challenge you to find a way to connect to their interest and understand their desires.

Fathers, teach your sons to be real men, to stand up for what's right and to shun the wrong. Teach them to respect themselves, women and others. Teach them to always do their best, to eat right and take care of their body, mind and spirit. Teach them to love and respect God and to follow His commandments. Teach them how to be leaders and to always drive for success. Teach them to respect and protect their most precious seed and their destiny. Teach them that a good name is more valuable than gold and that human life is important. Teach them how to solve their problems through communication and understanding. Finally, teach them by being an excellent example!

Fathers, teach your daughters that they are Queens and are not to settle for less. Teach them how to say no to negative people and relationships. Teach them to love and respect themselves and that they do not need someone else to complete them. Let them know there is nothing impossible for them to do. Teach them to be their best and to walk in the strength of who they are. Teach them to take care of their body, mind and spirit. Teach them how to solve their problem through communication and understanding. Finally, teach them by being an excellent example as you treat their mother with kindness.

I challenge you as men to treat your wives, partners, former partners, your children's mothers with respect. Always respect her, even when the intimate relationship has ended. Remember, you may not be a couple anymore but you are a team. You may have divorced from your wife, but you never are to separate from your children. Finally, you must never ever treat one child better than the other.

I wish you enormous success as you rebuild and strengthen your most crucial relationship with your child. Remember, you are not strong if they are weak. You are not a success, if they are failing. There is no success without a successor. We have children so they can continue us, they are an extension of us. They should reflect a life well lived. They are our today and tomorrow, but they can never represent you if they don't know you! They can never understand who they are if you are absent. They will thrive if you survive.

****

Remember, the only thing final in life is death, everything else is open for adjustment!

****

Thank you for this great honor, to share with you my joys, my hurts, my pain, my failures, and my remarkable successes. I have learned that being a father is the greatest accomplishment to which I can aspire.

I am praying for you daily that God would give you clarity and understanding. May God, bless you and give you strength on your journey to be that great father I know you will be.

You are the Batteries!

ROBERT L. QUEEN JR.

****

A Prayer for Fathers

God grant me the understanding to be a good father, to live by your precepts and examples. Teach me to speak your word as a man of faith and strength, to walk in peace and understanding, to be a master communicator and a good listener. Grant me the patience to treat others with the same respect I desire to be treated with. Guide me so that I may know your voice and plan for my life, and allow me to be a positive role model for those who follow me for generations to come.

Bibliography

Capecci, John and Cage, Timothy. Activism-inspiration, advocacy, personal – story, storytelling. "The enormity of Problems"

Blankenhorn, David (1995). Fatherless America: Confronting our Most Urgent Social Problems, Basic Books publishing New York, NY, U. S. A.

"Whatever your Life's Work is do it Well" Martin Luther King, Jr. (n.d.). BrainyQuote.com. Retrieved October 15, 2015, from BrainyQuote.com Web site: https://www.brainyquote.com/quotes/quotes/m/martin luth297529.html

Williamson, Marianne (1996). From the book A Return to Love: Reflections on the principles of "A course in Miracles" Harper Collins Publishers

Job, Steve. (2011) I Steve Jobs, in my own words - Agate Publishing –

Assisi, St Francis   Pre: (1226). "Start by Doing What's Necessary"

Wright, Lloyd Frank: Retrieved from Author frank Lloyd Wright Quotes -A-Z Quotes http://www.azquotes.com/quote/586359

Walter Lippmann. (n.d.). BrainyQuote.com. Retrieved June 26, 2017, from BrainyQuote.com Web site: https://www.brainyquote.com/quotes/quotes/w/walter lipp100564.html

Covey, Stephen R (1989). From the book 'The Habits of Highly Effective People" Habit 2 Begin with The End in Mind

Erickson Erikson's stages of psychosocial development, Retrieved from Verywell website November 23, 2015 https://www.verywell.com/erik-erikson-biography-1902-1994-2795538

Johnson, Samuel (1759). "Nothing will ever be attempted" Samuel Johnson. (n.d.). BrainyQuote.com. Retrieved September 26, 2015, from BrainyQuote.com Web site: https://www.brainyquote.com/quotes/quotes/s/samuel john122057.html

Carnegie, Dale "Most of the Important Things" Dale Carnegie. (n.d.). BrainyQuote.com. Retrieved May 6, 2015, from BrainyQuote.com Web site: https://www.brainyquote.com/quotes/quotes/d/daleca rneg100661.html

"Excellence is a Habit" Aristotle Quotes Will Durant. (n.d.). BrainyQuote.com. Retrieved May, 15, 2015 from BrainyQuote.com Web site: https://www.brainyquote.com/quotes/quotes/w/willdu rant145967.html

Clarke, Arthur C "Limits of the Possible" Quotes by Arthur C Clarke. (n.d.). BrainyQuote.com. Retrieved August 10, 2015, from BrainyQuote.com Web site: https://www.brainyquote.com/quotes/quotes/a/arthurc cl121735.html

Swindoll, Charles 'The Attitude" by Charles Swindoll. (n.d.). BrainyQuote.com. Retrieved August 20, 2015, from BrainyQuote.com Web site: https://www.brainyquote.com/quotes/quotes/c/charles rs165824.html

Hinkley, Gordon B. (1986) Retrieved October 4, 2015 from AZ quote website: <a href="http://www.azquotes.com/quote/586359" go title="Gordon B. Hinckley quote

Bryant, Paul: Bear Bryant on "Winners and Winning" Retrieved November 23, 2015 from qb website http://quotationsbook.com/quote/41439/

Counseling Center for Human Development University of Florida, American Psychologist Association, Dr. Miriam Stoppard. Retrieved October 2016 from Babble Web site: https://www.babble.com/pregnancy/anger-affecting-unborn-child/

National Center for Education Statistics. October 1997. Fathers' Involvement in Their Children's Schools; National Household Education Survey. NCES 98-091R2. Washington, D.C.: U.S. Department of Education Retrieved November 2016 from National Responsible Fatherhood Clearinghouse Web site: https://www.fatherhood.gov/content/dad-stats

National Association for Music Education, "Music and The Unborn Child" Retrieved 2017 from NAFME Web site: https://nafme.org/

Popenoe, Dr. David, January 1996 "Life Without Father" Significance of A Father's Influence. Retrieved November 2016 from Focus on the Family Web site: focusonthefamily.com

All Scripture quotations, unless otherwise indicated, are from the authorized King James Version (KJV), Public domain

94960740R00063

Made in the USA
Columbia, SC
05 May 2018